CAMBRIDGE LIBRARY COLLECTION

Books of enduring scholarly value

Literary Studies

This series provides a high-quality selection of early printings of literary works, textual editions, anthologies and literary criticism which are of lasting scholarly interest. Ranging from Old English to Shakespeare to early twentieth-century work from around the world, these books offer a valuable resource for scholars in reception history, textual editing, and literary studies.

Piozziana

Highly educated and accustomed to intellectual society, the writer and woman of letters Hester Lynch Piozzi (1741–1821) became a close friend of Samuel Johnson through her first husband, the brewer Henry Thrale. Her second marriage, to the Italian musician Gabriel Mario Piozzi in 1784, estranged her from Johnson, but following his death she published her groundbreaking *Anecdotes of the Late Samuel Johnson*, anticipating Boswell's biography. As well as her letters, poetry, essays, memoirs and travel diaries (several of which are also reissued in the Cambridge Library Collection), she was one of the first women to produce works on philology and history. Originally published in 1833, this highly readable volume of recollections by the writer and translator Edward Mangin (1772–1852) draws on her letters to him and his family (as well as on other memorabilia), extracts from which are quoted extensively in the work.

Cambridge University Press has long been a pioneer in the reissuing of out-of-print titles from its own backlist, producing digital reprints of books that are still sought after by scholars and students but could not be reprinted economically using traditional technology. The Cambridge Library Collection extends this activity to a wider range of books which are still of importance to researchers and professionals, either for the source material they contain, or as landmarks in the history of their academic discipline.

Drawing from the world-renowned collections in the Cambridge University Library and other partner libraries, and guided by the advice of experts in each subject area, Cambridge University Press is using state-of-the-art scanning machines in its own Printing House to capture the content of each book selected for inclusion. The files are processed to give a consistently clear, crisp image, and the books finished to the high quality standard for which the Press is recognised around the world. The latest print-on-demand technology ensures that the books will remain available indefinitely, and that orders for single or multiple copies can quickly be supplied.

The Cambridge Library Collection brings back to life books of enduring scholarly value (including out-of-copyright works originally issued by other publishers) across a wide range of disciplines in the humanities and social sciences and in science and technology.

Piozziana

Or, Recollections of the Late Mrs Piozzi

EDITED BY EDWARD MANGIN

CAMBRIDGE
UNIVERSITY PRESS

CAMBRIDGE UNIVERSITY PRESS

Cambridge, New York, Melbourne, Madrid, Cape Town,
Singapore, São Paolo, Delhi, Mexico City

Published in the United States of America by Cambridge University Press, New York

www.cambridge.org
Information on this title: www.cambridge.org/9781108057325

This edition first published 1833
This digitally printed version 2013

ISBN 978-1-108-05732-5 Paperback

—

PIOZZIANA.

without him We shall scarce sing
Bannissons la Melancholie ___ & hewill
scarce be led to translate it for us & say

From Your charming Voice and Eyes
Cupid's Darts new Mischief borrow;
And my Bosom heaves with Sighs
Whilst I sing— Lets banish Sorrow.

But still my lips refuse to say Farewell!
For in that Word— that fatal Word— howeer,
We promise hope & trust; We feel Despair.

Lord Byron.

Yours ever most faithfully

H. L. Piozzi

Bath
30: June 1817.

PIOZZIANA;

OR,

RECOLLECTIONS OF THE LATE
MRS. PIOZZI,

WITH REMARKS.

———◆———

BY

A FRIEND.

Perception quick, and luxury of thought.
   *   *   *   *
And spirits light to every joy in tune,
  And Friendship, ardent as a summer's noon,
  And conscious Honour's keen, instinctive sense,
  And smiles unforced, and easy confidence,
  And vivid Fancy.
MRS. BARBAULD.

LONDON:
EDWARD MOXON, DOVER STREET.
——
1833.

PIOZZIANA.

I HAVE now lived long, and though I have suffered somewhat, I have enjoyed much of what constitutes the pleasure of existence: but among the " changes and chances " which have fallen to my share, I cannot remember anything which proved a higher source of indulgence to me than my intimacy with the late Mrs. Piozzi.

My object in writing the following recollections of her is, to afford myself the gratification of recording all I can, of scenes and circumstances of a most agreeable kind; not without a hope of contributing, in some degree, to the amusement of others, who may be at the trouble to peruse my memoranda.

I pen these without confining my undertaking to any very methodical plan, and prescribe to myself

B

scarcely any other limits than those of truth. But before I proceed to my chief subject, I crave permission of my reader to offer an observation in defence of what is properly termed, but very improperly condemned as such,—egotism. Egotism it needs must be in a writer who uses the personal pronoun I; yet surely nothing more enhances the value of any narrative, than that same consequential pronoun. But a man who says " I did," " I saw," and " I heard," is not, on that account, to be stigmatized as an egotist. He must write or speak thus, in the spirit of vainglory, and self-approval; before the odium of coxcombry can justly attach to him; and even then, his statements are secure of being much more highly relished than if he had told his tale, like Julius Cæsar, or Lord Clarendon, in the third person singular. My heedless style of writing will probably not be found palatable; but what may be thought of it, is to me a matter of indifference : should my book prove welcome to the public, the public will be satisfied and so shall I; and not aiming at literary reputation, I am regardless of the censure which may be passed by critics on my performance.

Some apology may be considered requisite on another point; I mean for the apparent partiality, and occasionally an approach to compliment, discoverable in the letters of Mrs. Piozzi, addressed to myself and my family, from which I shall transcribe such portions as seem suited to my purpose. Mrs. Piozzi's nature was one of kindness; she derived pleasure from endeavouring to please; and if she perceived a moderately good quality in another, she generously magnified it into an excellence; while she appeared blind to faults and foibles, which could not have escaped the scrutiny of one possessing only half her penetration. But, as I have said, her disposition was kindly. It was so; and to such an extent, that during several years of familiar acquaintance with her, although I can recall many instances, I might say, hundreds, of her having spoken of the characters of others, I never heard one word of vituperation from her lips of any person who was the subject of discussion, except once when Baretti's name was mentioned. Of him she said that he was a bad man; but on my hinting a wish for particulars, after so heavy a charge, she seemed unwilling to explain herself, and spoke of him no

more. I may offer, as a further evidence of her
natural suavity, and of her freedom from those weak-
nesses, to which so many of both sexes are liable, the
following anecdote.

She, one evening, asked me abruptly if I did not
remember the scurrilous lines in which she had been
depicted by Gifford in his " Baviad and Mœviad."
And, not waiting for my answer, for I was indeed too
much embarrassed to give one quickly, she recited the
verses in question, and added, " how do you think
' Thrale's gray widow ' revenged herself? I contrived to get myself invited to meet him at supper at
a friend's house, (I think she said in Pall Mall), soon
after the publication of his poem, sat opposite to him,
saw that he was ' perplexed in the extreme;' and
smiling, proposed a glass of wine as a libation to our
future good fellowship. Gifford was sufficiently a man
of the world to understand me, and nothing could be
more courteous and entertaining than he was while
we remained together." This, it must be allowed,
was a fine trait of character, evincing thorough knowledge of life, and a very powerful mind.

Mrs. Piozzi can never be forgotten by the British

public, were it only because her name is closely connected with that of Johnson, whose reputation will
endure as long as the language—and the nation he
adorned. And were it possible that the most amusing
book ever written, Boswell's account of him, could have
dropped into neglect,— that now can never happen,—
Mr. Croker's edition of his entertaining work having
communicated new interest to his pages, on many of
which the accomplished editor's pen has shed light and
lustre. But fidelity obliged Mr. Croker to preserve unaltered, all that Boswell, &c., had accumulated respecting Mrs. P. in which there is not only a great proportion
of gossip, but of malignity and affected derision. My
wish is to exhibit her, or at least make her show herself
in a different and more favourable point of view, which
I hope to do in the course of this slight essay.

In direct contradiction to Boswell, Beloe, and
others, I venture to assert that it was not in the power
of any one who knew her to find aught in her character to despise, nor to refuse the meed of admiration
to her benevolence, her talents, and her acquirements,
or to the fascinating courtliness of her manners. The
worst which could be said of her, with truth, by the

moralist or the critic, is that some passages of her
life were marked by singularity; and that in her
(prose) writings especially, she frequently assumed a
childish style, to avoid, as I believe, being thought
laborious and pedantic. But, on the other hand, did
I contemplate a formal defence of her, I could bring
proofs in abundance, that various parts of her conduct,
in circumstances the most trying, were in rigid conformity to the principles of sound sense; and that the
world of letters has obligations to her for many a
beauteous page.

On the event of her death, which took place in
May, 1821, and in her eighty-second year, an article
was published in a Bristol newspaper, very well
written, and I apprehend, by Mrs. Pennington of the
Hot-wells, Clifton, in which her last words are mentioned. They are remarkable; and Mrs. Pennington
spoke to me of the scene on the awful occasion, as one
of the most striking imaginable. Mrs. Piozzi had
lain for some time silent, and as if exhausted, but
suddenly sat up, and with a piercing aspect, and slow
distinct utterance, said, " I die in the trust, and the
fear of God ! " Such words from such a person are

replete with meaning, and contain a lesson which
should not be forgotten; implying that neither confidence nor despair belonged properly to a reasoning
being who believed herself about to pass into a state
of everlasting existence. I feel, indeed, convinced
that had she possessed strength sufficient, she would
have gone farther into, and enlarged on, the subject
of her firm belief as a christian, and the ground of
that reliance which I know she had. It is to be
lamented that she did not, for she had much more
right to speak on religious topics, than many who
profess themselves theologians. She not only read
and wrote Hebrew, Greek, and Latin, but had for
sixty years constantly and ardently studied the Scrip-
tures, and the works of commentators, in the original
languages; and during her lengthened life conversed
with the soundest divines and best scholars of the age.
Being endowed with a most retentive memory, and
the rarest acuteness of understanding, she surely was
eminently qualified " to give a reason for the faith
that was in her."

   She had, however, to the close of her last illness,
her senses perfect, though unable to articulate; and

when in this state, was visited by her friend Sir George Smith Gibbes, so well known in Bath, and so much esteemed for his urbanity, his various attainments, extensive charities, and great professional skill.

Meeting Sir George in about a month after his farewell interview with her, he described to me a circumstance which took place on the awful occasion, of a nature too extraordinary to be disregarded or omitted in this record. When the dying lady saw him at her bed-side, she signified by her looks that she knew him well, and that neither his benevolence nor talents could be of any use; and, unable to speak, conveyed her mournful conviction of her situation, by tracing in the air with her extended hands, the exact outline of a coffin, and then lay calmly down.

It will naturally be expected that in writing of a female, and one so distinguished as Mrs. Piozzi, I should mention her personal appearance, but it is not easy to describe it. She was short, and though well-proportioned, broad, and deep-chested. Her hands were muscular and almost coarse, but her writing was, even in her 80th year, exquisitely beautiful; and one day, while conversing with her on the subject of education, she observed that " all Misses now a-days, wrote so like each other, that it was provoking ; " adding, " I love to see individuality of character, and abhor sameness, especially in what is feeble and flimsy." Then, spreading her hand, she said, " I believe I owe what you are pleased to call my good writing, to the shape of this hand, for my uncle, Sir Robert Cotton, thought it was too manly to be employed in writing like a boarding-school girl; and so I came by my vigorous, black manuscript."

Her countenance is constantly in my recollection ; but could I have forgotten it, I should have been reminded of its striking features by a good miniature of her in my possession. This was her gift to me, in her 77th year, accompanied by some lines, of her own composition, enclosed in the case containing this valuable memorial. She gave the ingenious artist, Roche of Bath, many sittings; and enjoined him to make the painting in all respects a likeness; to take care to show her face deeply rouged, which it always was ; and to introduce a trivial deformity of the lower jaw on the left side, where she told me she had been severely hurt by her horse treading on her as she lay prostrate, after being thrown in Hyde Park. This miniature is, in the essential of resemblance, perfect; as all who recollect the original, her very erect carriage, and most expressive face, could attest.

Sometimes, when she favoured me and mine with a visit, she used to look at her little self, as she called it, and speak drolly of what she once was, as if talking of some one else; and one day, turning to me, I remember her saying, "no, I never was handsome; I had always too many strong points in my face for beauty." I ventured to express a doubt of this, and said that Doctor Johnson was certainly an admirer of her personal charms. She replied that she believed his devotion was at least as warm towards the table and the table-talk at Streatham. This was, as is well known, Mrs. Thrale's place of residence in the country. I was tempted to observe that I thought, as I still do, that Johnson's anger on the event of her second marriage was excited by some feeling of disappointment; and that I suspected he had formed hopes of attaching her to himself. It would be disingenuous on my part to attempt to repeat her answer:

I forget it; but the impression on my mind is that she did not contradict me.

Conversing on her appearance when young, she mentioned an extraordinary fact, the particulars of which I, long after, communicated to the public, in a letter to the Editor of the " Gentleman's Magazine;" the substance may be repeated here. She inquired if I had ever seen, when in Dublin, a painting by Hogarth, in the splendid library of the Earl of Charlemont, and which had been executed by the renowned artist for the father of the present peer; it was called "the Lady's last Stake." I said I had never seen the picture, but had heard of it often, and remembered some notice of it in Ireland's Hogarth: when she proceeded to state, as nearly as I can recollect, that one evening Hogarth called on her uncle Cotton, with whom she lived; and seeing her, then a girl of about fourteen, examined her countenance studiously, and addressed her, saying, "stay quiet until I make a memorandum of your face." This he did in his pocket-book, observing, that " he would put her into a picture, the subject of which would be a lesson to her to avoid the danger arising from deep play; and

that when finished, she should see what he had done."
After a lapse of some weeks, Hogarth paid another
visit, and then exhibited " the Lady's last Stake."
" But," said Mrs. P., " he had scarcely attempted a
likeness, having made his rash lady a beauty; and
there's the history of this very clever work of the
famous painter." Since the appearance of my letter
in the " Gentleman's Magazine," a splendid engraving, in mezzo-tinto, of the above-mentioned painting
has been published.

Of her erudition, and the powers of her mind, I
find it difficult to speak so as to satisfy myself, yet
meet, in some degree, what I believe to be the
opinion of others.

Making every allowance for Boswell's insinuations,
and Gifford's satire, it might be too much to say that
she appeared a scholar and a wit in the eyes of a
judge so formidable as Johnson. I confess I thought
her both; and indeed cannot avoid believing that even
Johnson highly appreciated her talents and accom-
plishments; he was shamefully insincere if he did
not. Many proofs might be adduced that she knew
more of books, and possessed larger stores of appli-

cable literature and entertaining anecdote, than most females, or than several of the other sex, who have been generally and greatly extolled. But, a reference to one of her literary labours, which fell under my own observation, will answer the purpose of showing that she had pretensions, and of no ordinary kind, to the character of a learned and ingenious writer.

Early in the year 1815, I called on her, then resident in New King Street, Bath, to examine, by her desire, a manuscript which she informed me she was preparing for the press. After a short general conversation, we sat down to a table on which lay two manuscript volumes, one of them, the fair copy of her work, in her own incomparably fine hand-writing. The title was "Lyford Redivivus;" the idea being taken from a diminutive old volume, printed, if I do not forget, in 1657, and professing to be an alphabetical account of the names of men and women, and their derivations. Her work was somewhat on this plan: the christian or first name given, Charity, for instance, followed by its etymology; anecdotes of the eminent or obscure, who have borne the appellation;

applicable epigrams, biographical sketches, short poetical illustrations, &c.

I read over twelve or fourteen articles, and found them exceedingly interesting; abounding in spirit, and in what to my very limited knowledge appeared novelty; and all supported by quotations in Hebrew, Greek, Latin, Italian, French, Celtic and Saxon. There was a learned air over all I read; and in every page, much information, ably compressed, and forming what I should have supposed, an excellent popular volume. She was now seventy-five; and I naturally complimented her, not only on the work in question, but the amazing beauty and variety of her handwriting. She seemed gratified, allowed me to make a few extracts, and desired me to mention the MS. to some London publisher. This I afterwards did, and sent the work to one alike distinguished for discernment and liberality, but with whom we could not come to an arrangement. I have heard no more of " Lyford Redivivus" since, and know not in whose hands the MS. may now be. The following copy of one of my extracts, will give a general idea of the work, though by no means the most favourable.

"BELINDA.

"The name is familiar to our fancy since Pope's elegant letter to Miss Fermor, preceding his beautiful poem, the Rape of the Lock. The appellation is appropriate to any much admired damsel; admired for her personal charms I mean; we could in no wise endure an ugly, or an awkward Belinda.

"Meanwhile, a lady of quality once gave her friend, (Mrs. Piozzi means that the gift was to herself; she still had it in her possession ;) a little chest for tea, made of the willow-tree Pope planted at Twickenham, in the year 1715; which Lady Howe cut down four-score years after; and the people cried shame, and struggled for bits of it. But, said a gentleman, there should be two words on the box, methinks, to tell what it is, or nobody will guess at its value, or its oddity; only just two words. I know, said another, no two words that would explain the matter, unless they were *tu doces*—thou tea-chest. This raised a laugh; and Lady K. requesting she might be let into the jest, if there were any; one of us, (Mrs. Piozzi, who wrote

them ;) sent her these verses in the morning, from
a rough rock in North-Wales, where the box was
intended to reside.

"Thou Tea-chest! form'd from Pope's fam'd willow,
  Which served our poet for his pillow,
  When round his head gay visions rose
  Of bright Belinda, and her beaux ;
  Torn from thy Thames, to scenes thus rude,
  How much of life's vicissitude—
            Thou tea-chest!

" Presented by a noble dame,
  From thee I hop'd inspiring flame,
  But no : that Indian shrub alone
  Which at thy birth was scarcely known,
  In fragrant fumes of fresh bohea,
  Is all I can inhale from thee,
            Thou tea-chest!"

"METHUSELAH

has been long recorded and renowned for having
lived more years than were ever permitted to any
other mortal.   Lyford says he begged for death.   No
wonder, having existed through nine centuries !   But
the meaning of his name has been variously explained.

Rowlands, to whom I referred under the article, Enosh, exhibits a surprising chain of ideas applicable to the names of the ten Patriarchs from Adam to Noah inclusive, thus.

ADAM	Man.
SETH	Set, or placed.
ENOSH	In misery.
KAINAN . . .	Lamenting.
MAHALEEL . .	Blessed God.
JARED	Shall come down.
ENOCH. . . .	Teaching.
METHUSELAH .	That his death will send.
LAMECH . . .	To humbled, smitten man.
NOAH	Consolation."

" JOB,

oppressed by enemies. His three daughters, Jemima, the dawn; Kezia, a struggle with poverty; Keren-happuk, the horn of abundance."

" MADOC,

Derived from the Celtic Ma-du-ux. *Dux* has been

always a leader, a conductor. There came out a book some twenty-five years ago, about 1790, giving an account of the tribes of North Wales, where these long departed princes were faithfully recorded by the names of *Ma'-doc*, and *Fa'-doc*, and *Cur-ogie*; but a wicked wag from London crying out, ' What's here ? a history of mad-dog, and fat-dog, and *cur-ogey*,'—drove names, and book, and all away, till Mr. Southey called them again into notice.''

In general society Mrs. Piozzi was retiring and reserved; at least as reserved as is consistent with good-breeding, of which she was a perfect mistress.

In large assemblies, at her own house, or elsewhere, she talked, but in a subdued tone, and only on common topics; for she knew the world of politeness too well not to remember that absolute silence is as vulgar and vexatious, as loquacity, or claiming too much attention to ourselves, would be.

In familiar conversation with a few intimates, she was animated and interesting, certainly beyond any person I ever met. She excelled in the delicate art

of exciting and encouraging others to talk; quickly
discovered the points on which each was most likely
to be best informed, and would then either express
her wish to one of the party, to be better acquainted
with such or such particulars, or put a question, as if
she actually did want information.

She attended eagerly to the expected reply; and
seemed so grateful for the communication made to
her, that the person appealed to felt himself for the
time in a state of superiority to the inquirer.   In fact
she perpetually contrived to appear at first less learned
than she really was; and not only avoided hurting
any one's self-love, but had the ingenuity to augment
it, and afford others the triumph of thinking that their
agreeableness was the cause of hers!

She told a story incomparably well; omitting every
thing frivolous or irrelevant, accumulating all the important circumstances, and after a short pause (her
aspect announcing that there was yet more to come),
finished with something new, pointed, and brilliant.

To render all this more fascinating, she would
throw into her narrative a gentle imitation — not
mimicry, of the parties concerned, at which they

might themselves have been present without feeling
offended.

In this way she once, I remember, gave us two
scenes; one at Streatham and the other, I think, in
London; both infinitely interesting, but for different
reasons; and rendered surprisingly dramatic by her
mode of relating what passed. The first referred to
one of Johnson's eccentric habits. A large company
had just sat down to the dinner-table, where Johnson's chair was, however, still vacant; for, though the
Doctor had been heard descending the stairs, he was
not yet withinside the door, " So," said Mrs. P., " I
supposed there was something wrong, and making
my excuses, started up, and ran in search of my
loiterer; and there was he in the passage, indulging
in one of his strange whims; stepping forward, drawing back his leg, and then another step! I scolded
him soundly; not for affectation, nor absence of mind,
for, to do him justice, of all such absurdities he was
incapable; but for pursuing a queer practice at a time
when others were waiting. At length I got him in;
and after dinner he made us ample amends by his
talk, as he did invariably." In telling this, she bent

her neck sideways, looked solemn, and stepped to and fro, so as to transmit, I have no doubt, a very good notion of Johnson's air.

The other anecdote to which I have alluded is altogether exceedingly curious; involving a serious charge against Johnson's dignity of mind; and that of another equally distinguished man. I should observe that this was told to me, when but two or three of those most intimate with the narrator were present. I had remarked to her that Johnson's readiness to condemn any moral deviation in others was, in a man so entirely before the public as he was, nearly a proof of his own spotless purity of conduct. She said, " Yes, Johnson was, on the whole, a rigid moralist; but he could be ductile, I may say, servile; and I will give you an instance. We had a large dinner-party at our house; Johnson sat on one side of me, and Burke on the other; and in the company there was a young female (Mrs. Piozzi named her), to whom I, in my peevishness, thought Mr. Thrale superfluously attentive, to the neglect of me and others; especially of myself, then near my confinement, and dismally low-spirited; notwithstanding

which, Mr. T. very unceremoniously begged of me
to change place with Sophy ———, who was threat-
ened with a sore-throat, and might be injured by
sitting near the door. I had scarcely swallowed a
spoonful of soup when this occurred, and was so over-
set by the coarseness of the proposal, that I burst into
tears, said something petulant—that perhaps ere long,
the lady might be at the head of Mr. T.'s table,
without displacing the mistress of the house, &c., and
so left the apartment. I retired to the drawing-room,
and for an hour or two contended with my vexation,
as I best could, when Johnson and Burke came up.
On seeing them, I resolved to give a *jobation* to both,
but fixed on Johnson for my charge, and asked him
if he had noticed what passed, what I had suffered,
and whether, allowing for the state of my nerves, I
was much to blame? He answered, ' Why, possibly
not; your feelings were outraged.' I said, ' Yes,
greatly so; and I cannot help remarking with what
blandness and composure you *witnessed* the outrage.
Had this transaction been told of others, your anger
would have known no bounds; but, towards a man
who gives good dinners, &c, you were meekness

itself!' Johnson coloured, and Burke, I thought,
looked foolish; but I had not a word of answer from
either."

GHOSTS.

THE subject of ghosts and apparitions is one which
has engaged almost every class of mind, from the
highest to the least enlightened.   On one occasion I
introduced it before her, from a strong desire to ascer-
tain her way of thinking on the question of superstition; being persuaded that I should hear something
ingenious from her; something which would be neither an imbecile admission of her belief in ghosts, &c.,
nor a gross and vulgar condemnation of those who
hold that the departed are allowed to revisit this
earthly scene.   She accordingly enlarged very amus-
ingly on stories of preternatural appearances; told
several good ones which she had heard and read,
showed how much of *national* character might be
traced in popular credulity of every kind, and ended
by declaring that her opinion was precisely in accord-

ance with mine. This, however startling at first, is
nevertheless such as must be that of any one who
takes the trouble to reflect; and it is that all, or nearly
all, the ghost stories commonly related, are, in the
strictest sense of the word, *true*. She maintained
seriously, and with much argument happily applied,
that these tales of apparitions are narratives of *waking
dreams*, to which we are as liable as to those that
occupy the imagination in sleep; and that when a
man tells how he saw one known to be dead, or at
the moment possibly five hundred miles off, he either
mistook one object of vision for another; or absolutely
did see, in a *waking dream*, the subject of his rela-
tion ; and that there was no violation of moral truth
in either of these supposed cases. The want of veracity in the ordinary relaters of such stories, is to be
found among those who *repeat* the statements of the
original dreamer. She was convinced, as I am, that
a disordered state of the stomach, or something irregular in the circulation of the blood, was the main
cause alike of sight-seeing during sleep, and of dreams
by day, and when the visionary is broad awake. She
made many pertinent and curious remarks on this

subject; one of which was that the sleeper who, in the night, saw forms and colours in his dream, was so much under the dominion of delusion as to imagine that it was light, when in fact it was dark; and that there was no reason to be assigned for the powers of fancy not being as great in a waking as a sleeping state. She then repeated the particulars of a spectre seen by (I think she said) *Miles Andrews,* and which have been differently told elsewhere; but she assured me, *on her word,* that she had the circumstances as I shall report them, from the *sight-seer's* own mouth.

It seems that Lord Lyttelton, meeting Andrews in a street in London, informed him that he intended him a visit such a day, at his country residence, not far from town. Andrews gladly heard of this, and left London to prepare for the reception of his noble friend. The day, and the dinner hour came, but not Lord L., nor any message from him. His host to no purpose waited, sat up beyond his general time of retiring, and at length went to bed, leaving lights burning when he lay down. In a few minutes afterwards, and while yet wide awake, he saw Lord L. wearing his well-known dressing-gown, and seated in

a chair at the farther extremity of the room; on which
he upbraided him for the disappointment his neglect
had inflicted on him, and jocularly scolded him for the
frolic he had indulged in, desiring him to go to his
own room, and leave him to his repose. Lord Lyttelton at that instant rose, and, as Andrews concluded,
glided behind a large arm-chair.

He now rang the bell for his confidential servant,
and desired him to make fast the doors, and go to
rest, since Lord L. was at last in the house. The
servant, staring, said that could not be, as he had
locked all the doors some hours before, and that
assuredly his lordship had not arrived. Andrews told
the astonished man what he had seen and said; and
rising, proceeded with him to the apartment usually
assigned to Lord L., and elsewhere through the house,
but found him not. Next day Andrews went to town,
and finding Lord Lyttelton confined by indisposition,
repeated his wonderful history to him; but the other
solemnly declared he had not left his room since they
met in —— street, having been ill; and observed,
that he had not sent an excuse, as too ceremonious.
This is nearly as *good* a ghost-story as can well be *got*

up; yet manifestly the vision was the result of a *waking dream,* suggested by the anxiety of the expectant for the wished-for visit of his accomplished guest.

PEDIGREE.

HAVING had a conversation with her on antiquity of families, and her own descent, I received from Mrs. Piozzi the following letter. I cherish the original as a document of great value :—

" Charles Sixth of France
Married Isabella of Bavaria :
Their daughter Katherine married Henry V. of England ;
And after his death, Owen Tudor ;
by whom she had *three sons.*
The first of these, Edmund Earl of Richmond.
was father to Henry VII.
The *second* was Jasper Earl of Pembroke ;
The *third* was *Fychan* Tudor de Berayne ;
His son married Jasper's daughter ;
and
Had an only child ; who, wedding
Constance D' Aubigné,
favourite Lady to Anne de Bretagne,
was father to the famous Heiress,
Katherine Tudor de Berayne,

Cousin and ward to Queen Elizabeth,
And who, with her Majesty's express approbation,
Married Sir John Salusbury of Lleweney.
When he died, she was addressed
by Maurice Wynne of Gwydir,
as she returned from following her husband to the grave,
and told him she had engaged herself to Sir Richard Clough,
but that if she was unfortunate enough to survive him,
She consented to be Lady Gwydir ;
and so she was :
and after Maurice Wynne's death, wedded
Thelwall of Plas y Ward
and with *his, her* bones repose.

Her *heart* lies buried, by her own command, with that of her
second husband, who died at Antwerp (but *whose heart* was
brought to Wales and interred with hers). Her estate was settled
by her guardian, Queen Elizabeth, on her first husband, Sir John
Salusbury of Lleweney,

Whose son, surnamed Sir John the Strong, married Lady Ur-
sula Stanley, Dowager Countess of Derby ; and *their* son, at a
very advanced age, had only one daughter, by a Miss Myddelton,
Hester Salusbury ; who marrying Sir Robert Cotton, of Com-
bermere, transferred the name and estate to *their* son, who
wedded Philadelphia *Lynch*, and was, by *her*, father to Hester
Maria Cotton, by marriage Hester Maria *Salusbury*, and the
incomparable mother of an only child, your friend,

Hester Lynch Piozzi.

Meanwhile,

Katherine de Berayne, after the death of Sir John Salusbury,
married Sir Richard Clough, and had by him *two daughters*, one

of whom married Wynne of Melai, and is ancestress to Lord Newborough. The other married Roger Salusbury of Bachy Graig, youngest brother of Sir John Salusbury of Lleweney, between whose ages there were sixteen years, I have been told. Their son by him married a Myddleton of Chirk Castle, and their son John married a Miss Norris of Speke.

Their son Thomas married Bridget Percival,

and

their son married Mary Pennant of Downing ;

their son married Lucy Salusbury, his uncle's daughter ;

and

their son was father by Hester Maria Cotton,

to

Hester Lynch Piozzi.

Thus Katherine de Berayne obtained the appellation of Mam y Cymry, mother of Wales ; having had offspring by all her four husbands, and connecting them each with the other. My uncle sold the Berayne estate to Hughes, the rich possessor of the Parys copper mine in Anglesea, and the Lleweney estate to Lord Kirkwall's father—Fitzmaurice, who married the Countess of Orkney. His son has since sold poor Lleweney itself to the same Mr. Hughes, who has pulled down the venerable mansion built 1000 years ago ; and my heart bled to see its ruin, when I was in Denbighshire last August, 1816.

And now I think here is tediousness enough."

ANCIENT VASES, &c.

ONE day, paying a visit to her, at her house in Gay Street, Bath, she showed me a small cabinet of china ware, &c. Among other articles of the collection, were two vases of baked clay; one about twelve, the other, perhaps fifteen inches high, externally black and glazed. The smaller vase was plain; the other, and larger, distinguished by rude figures in relief, somewhat resembling Pegasus, and other forms; both in perfect preservation, and probably designed for holding wine. She stated that they were presented to her by Count Visconti; that she returned him her thanks for such fine *antiques*, and that the count replied that they were indeed such, having been *antiques* in the time of Cicero, in the ruins of whose villa of *Tusculanum* they were found. They were Etruscan, she presumed, and of an age before *Romulus*, and possibly almost three thousand years old. She also exhibited a pair of china bottles, adorned with mouth-pieces and hoops of silver, which had been four hundred years in the possession of her family, and were brought from the East by early navigators, before the discovery of the Cape of Good-Hope, and when the voyage from Europe lasted three years.

BATTLE OF BOSWORTH.

PASSING an evening with her in October, 1816, she entertained her company with several stories, and among them, told the following. She said, that in the family of *Mostyn*, in Denbighshire, with whom she was connected, she had frequently seen a golden cup, the history of which was repeated to her by the present possessor.

King Henry VII., when Earl of Richmond, and on his way to fight Richard the Third at Bosworth, stopped for a day at Mostyn-hall; and on leaving, told Lady Mostyn that, should he be victorious, as he hoped to be, he would, when the battle was over, send her his *sword* by a special messenger, whom he should despatch from the field. He won the day, and sent the sword, as he promised; and for ages it hung in the armoury at *Mostyn*. But a good old lady of the family at length observing that the hilt was of pure gold, and exclaiming that it was a pity metal of such value should lie useless, had the handle melted down, and converted into a caudle-cup. The *blade* was lost.

MRS. SIDDONS.

I possess, in the hand-writing of Mrs. Piozzi, the following *impromptu*, on hearing Mrs. Siddons read passages from the Paradise Lost; by Sir William Weller Pepys, Bart.

" When Siddons reads from Milton's page,
    Then sound and sense unite;
Her varying tones our hearts engage,
    With exquisite delight :

" So well these varying tones accord
    With his seraphic strain,
We hear, we feel in ev'ry word
    His Angels speak again."

GARTH THE POET.

In June, 1817, I received a billet from her, in which she says, " here is the very passage that seduced

me to believe the lines were written by Dryden."
This communication refers to a passage in Bowles's
edition of Pope's works; vol. i. page 312, note on
verse 122 of the " Rape of the Lock." " *Each silver
vase.*" *Parnell* accidentally hearing Pope repeat the
description of the toilette, privately turned the lines
into monkish-latin verses; and Pope, to whom he
immediately communicated them, was astonished at
the resemblance, till Parnell undeceived him. Mr.
Harte told me that Dryden had been imposed on by
a similar little stratagem. One of his friends translated into Latin verse, printed and pasted on the
bottom of an old hat-box, that celebrated passage—

" To die is landing on some silent shore," &c.

and that Dryden, on opening the box, was alarmed
and amazed.—WARTON.

This, I observed to Mrs. Piozzi, who had mentioned the supposed fact, is some mistake on the
part of *Harte*, or *Warton ;* the passage being in the
third part of Garth's " Dispensary ;" but the story
might be true of *Garth.*

CONVERSATION.

1815.

WE were talking of books generally, when she spoke in the highest possible terms of *Walter Scott;* and said he was a great and extraordinary being, had revived the spirit of poetry, and added lustre to his age and country. She did not treat *Lord Byron* with much respect as a writer; but broke away into encomiums on *Mackenzie*, the author of " the Man of Feeling," &c.; and said she was charmed with the title lately given him by the *unknown* author of the new novel, " Waverley;" and that *Mackenzie* was indeed " the Addison of Scotland."

She added that she had passed some happy hours in Edinburgh; and was delighted to find there, in the language, style of building, and general manners, so many vestiges of France, introduced, no doubt, in the days of the hapless *Mary*.

She greatly admired, she said, the Scottish people, admitting that I was right in observing, as I did to compliment her, that *Boswell* was an obtuse man, and did not understand *Johnson*, when he represents him

as malevolently disposed towards Scotland; while, in
fact, his sarcastic mode of speaking of that nation,
was only *his* way of being facetious. This led her to
remark that she knew the famous *John Wilkes* well,
and had often enjoyed his fine " conversation talents."
She recalled the droll retort of *Wilkes*, when he one
day overheard *Johnson* enlarging on the subject of
human freedom, and cried out, " What is the man
saying? *Liberty* sounds as oddly in *his* mouth, as
Religion would in *mine!*"

Reverting to *Mackenzie*, she said she did not, any
more than Doctor *Johnson*, think highly of his " Man
of the World;" and that *Johnson*, whose name she
frequently introduced, was the reverse of illiberal with
regard to Scotland, or Scottish genius; for that he
perpetually took opportunities of applauding both;
and was one time speaking most praisingly of *Thomson*, when a Scotch gentleman came in; on which
Johnson immediately desisted; and said afterwards,
that he " could not endure to hear *one Scot* magnify
another, which he knew would be the case."

I reminded her of what he so bitterly said of
another race of people, as distinguished from those

of Scotland; she laughed, and said that was very
bitterly *intended*. Speaking of France and Italy,
she observed that *Italy* was the most lovely region on
earth; yet, that while it had in it more splendid
remains of antiquity, and more beauties of every
kind, it had also more beggars, more dirt, and more
superstition, than all the rest of the world combined.
She professed that she dearly loved France, and
French habits; and said that in 1775, she passed some
most agreeable days in Paris, with her husband, *Mr.
Thrale ;* when he made acquaintance with *Santerre*,
with whom he wished to commune on the business of
their mutual calling, that of brewing: that at this time
there was a procession; and a noble horse belonging
to *Santerre* impeding the advance of the courtly train,
a military grandee of the royal party drew out a pistol
and shot the animal dead on the spot.   The act filled
Santerre with indignation, and (as Mrs. Piozzi was
convinced) made him what he subsequently proved,
a most inveterate revolutionist. It is well remembered
that *Santerre* commanded the national guard, on the
21st of January, 1793; and rode close to the scaffold
on which Louis XVI. perished.

She spoke with much pleasant affectation of jealousy, of Wales, her country; and said it was greatly neglected by historians, topographers, and antiquaries; for that the Principality had to boast, not only of infinite natural beauties, but of stores of human genius that the British language should not be allowed to decay, as she was afraid it would; but that it was not yet forgotten, as in the preceding summer she had heard the Church-service in *Welsh*, and " Brennin Sior," King George, prayed for. She observed, that the English, properly so called, though they had not any *music* to vaunt of, had a superabundance of *wit* in their proverbs, popular sayings, and caricatures; and remembered, for example, some years ago, a pungent but *untranslatable* toast in circulation, which she thought a genuine specimen of national humour; " God save the King;—the Prince of Wales *for ever!* " She showed me a very clever drawing, well coloured, of her place in Wales; which, she added, was almost in ruins, but had been put into repair by the care and generosity of her husband, *Mr. Piozzi*, of whom she invariably spoke with ardent affection and respect. In the course of talk, she said she presumed *Mackenzie's* " Man of

Feeling " to have been written *before Sterne* published
his " Sentimental Journey; " (which I ventured to
doubt,) and mentioned, as admirably well written, a
paper on *Spring* in the *Mirror ;* asking if I knew the
author. Strictly speaking I do not; but told her I had
heard that Essay attributed to the pen of an accomplished Irish gentleman of the name of Dickson, afterwards a physician, and, I believe, many years dead.

Speaking of *Scott,* she said his " *Marmion* " was a
fine poem, but that his best writing was to be—and probably always *would* be—found among the short pieces
of " Border Poetry," which he published first.

SIR JOSHUA REYNOLDS.

CONVERSING on the character of *Sir Joshua Reynolds,*
she, though a great admirer of the artist, told me this
story of him to prove what she asserted, that he was
imperfectly educated; and occasionally made her
start by betraying ignorance on points not directly
belonging to his profession.   He had painted a picture of two celebrated beauties of the time, sitting in

a garden, with a landscape in the distance. On the
seat in which the ladies were placed, he had inscribed,
" *et in Arcadia ego !*" which, said Mrs. Piozzi, he did
as not understanding the words; or at least their
application. They form the inscription on a *tomb* in
Gaspar Poussin's fine picture of Arcadia, intimating
that death was even in the region of innocence and
delight. This comment of hers she had communicated to Johnson, who, she assured me, agreed with
her as to the absurdity of what the great English
painter had done. But a gentleman who was present
when she repeated the above, suggested, as most probable, her having overlooked some circumstance in the
composition authorising Sir Joshua's introduction of
the Latin words in Poussin's picture. The sentence
is, I believe, not in Latin, but Italian.

ETYMOLOGY.

SHE was exceedingly fond of tracing words to their
sources, and had accumulated an immensity of odd
derivations. For instance, she one day told me that

the phrase *on tick* came from the following origin.
In Elizabeth's time, such persons as frequented the
theatres, *the Globe, the Curtain,* &c., in Southwark,
crossed from the city in boats, each receiving a ticket
from the waterman who ferried the parties over.
This was shown on retiring from the play in search
of their boats; so the proper boat attended, and they
who thus went and came were specified, for shortness,
as persons "*on tick,*" and who were *trusted* for the
payment of their fare till re-landed on their own side
of the river. She subjoined—" this etymology sounds
ridiculously—but, let any one find me a better."

JEMMY TWITCHER.

I ASKED her for the true cause of the name Jemmy
Twitcher, being given to *Lord Sandwich.* It will be
remembered that in "The Beggars' Opera," Act iii.
Scene 5, Macheath exclaims, "that *Jemmy Twitcher*
should 'peach me, I own surprised me." At the
tumultuous period of Wilkes's uproar, he, who had
been originally on terms of friendship with *Lord*

Sandwich, found in his lordship the chief instigator of government against him. Accordingly, when the opera was next performed, and *Beard,* the Macheath of the day, delivered the above-mentioned words, the people, recollecting the reported perfidy of *Lord S.* to his political friend *Wilkes,* their idol, and applying the sarcasm, fixed the title of *Jemmy Twitcher* on the great man. The nick-name is recorded in *Herbert Croft's* " Love and Madness," or, letters from *Hackman* to Miss *Martha Rae,* who lived with *Lord Sandwich.*

CHARADE.

SHE had a happy turn for the lighter sort of verse; and could, I am persuaded, have written a clever satirical epigram, that most difficult of poetical efforts; but her goodness of heart was greater even than her acuteness of observation. As a specimen of her playfulness, here is, from a copy given to me by herself, a *charade.*

> " Est totum flumen, caput aufer, splendet in armis ;
> Caudam deme, volat : viscera tolle, dolet."

" Translated and *amplified* for the ladies, by *Hester Lynch Piozzi.*

" In fluent streams my liquid *whole*
Is seen through foreign realms to roll ;
Cut off the tail, a bird shall rise,
Terror and boast of Indian skies :
Cut off the head, a hero shines
Immortalized in epic lines ;
Cut out the bowels, and a wound
Confest by Romans will be found ;
Close head and tail—no space between—
Your riddle's merit must be seen."

The word is Vulturnus, explained in Latin :

" Vulturnus flumen ; Turnus splendescit in armis ;
Avolat en Vultur ; vexat quoque corpora—Vulnus.

LETTER.—GRATTAN.

" *Tuesday Evening, October,* 2, 1816.

" I RETURN you, dear Sir, the only piece of writing
which could have waked me from the stupor of this
evening.   Doctor Gibbes will tell you to-morrow he
had made me take opium; and being no elephant, it
had subdued and calmed, not warmed and roused me
to the thoughts of *battle.*

"Your countryman's eloquence would, however, light up fire in mortals half dead, I think; at least if a spark was left within them. . . . . You did not mean to *give* it me, did you? remember I write in my sleep;

"H. L. P."

This letter refers to a pamphlet I had sent to her; the merit of which she was thoroughly capable of feeling. It was a printed copy of a speech delivered in the House of Commons, in May, 1815, in favour of war, by the never-dying Henry Grattan, and a splendid specimen of that great orator's peculiar power, by which he brings the most refined language, the richest imagery, and the closest logic, to bear upon his subject; while he is sublime, he is never obscure : and almost all his passages have the terseness of epigram. But it is to be lamented that the moral philosopher should thus be lost in the statesman, and that the atrocities and folly of war should, on *any* occasion, have found an advocate in such a man as *Grattan!*

Doctor Gibbes, so often mentioned in her correspondence, is the estimable man and distinguished physician, Sir George Smith Gibbes, of Bath, already noticed in these memoranda.

"THE FOUNTAINS," &c.

" WILL my kind patron read the enclosed to his
ladies? And will *they* tell me on Monday what *he*
thinks of it? But he is always partial to

          " His much obliged
                " H. L. P.

" He will be so well aware that this intrusion on
his good-nature is a mark of confidence in his friendship, that there is no need to say *show* it nobody. I
have longed to mention it, twenty times:—

> " But this is a thing the most oddest,
> Some folks are so plaguily modest, &c.
>   " *October* 25, 1816."

I *think* the above sprightly epistle alludes to a small
dramatic piece formed by Mrs. P. from the substance
of a fairy tale in French; and probably not thought
fit for the stage; but which appeared to me a very
pretty and ingenious production; it was, however,
quickly and conscientiously restored to the writer;
nor can I now tell what became of the manuscript,
no more than I can what was the fate of another

work of her pen, of incalculable value to such readers
as are fond of anecdote; i. e., nine-tenths of such
as read at all. I called on her one day, and at an
early hour by her desire; when she showed me a
heap of what are termed pocket-books, and said she
was sorely embarrassed on a point, upon which she
condescended to say she would take my advice.
" You see in that collection," she continued, " a
diary of mine of more than *fifty* years of my life : I
have scarcely omitted *any* thing which occurred to me
during the time I have mentioned ; my books contain
the conversation of every person of almost every class
with whom I have held intercourse ; my remarks on
what was said ; down-right facts, and scandalous *on
dits ;* personal portraits, and anecdotes of the characters concerned; criticisms on the publications and
authors of the day, &c. Now I am approaching the
grave, and agitated by doubts as to what I should do
—whether burn my manuscripts, or leave them to
futurity? Thus far, my decision is to *destroy* my
papers; shall I, or shall I not?"

I took the freedom of saying, " By no means do
an act, which done cannot be amended; keep your

papers safe from prying eyes; and at last, trust them
to the discretion of survivors." Her answer was that,
at least for the present, they were rescued from the
flames; and so saying, she replaced the numerous
volumes in her cabinet. I did not see the inside of
one of them, and, of course, can say nothing from my
own knowledge of the contents; but cannot doubt
that they were, in all respects, most interesting. I
am led to think this from recollecting the character of
her mind; the eagerness with which she sought the
society of the distinguished in her day; the elevated
circles in which she was privileged to move; the
closeness of observation with which she viewed life
and manners, and her wondrous strength of memory.
To wish that the reading world should be put in possession of *all* she had gathered, might be extravagant;
but undoubtedly many portions of her *Diaries* would
have admitted of publication, and been perused with
avidity.

STANZAS.

THE lines which follow are, I suppose, by her; but the copy which I have before me in her handwriting, is unaccompanied by any letter or memorandum to assist my recollection. I can only conjecture that they are referred to in a note, without date, addressed to myself, in which Mrs. P. says, " It is come into my head that dear Mr. ——— recollected something of these lines this morning. *I* only recollect our conversation dissipating the gloom *they* were born in, about this time two years. If liked, they will do for a scrap-book."

" Is it of intellectual pow'rs,
   Which time develops, time devours,
   Which *twenty* years perhaps are ours,
      That man is vain?

" Of such the infant shows no sign,
   And childhood dreads the dazzling shine
   Of knowledge-bright in rays divine,
      As mental pain.

" Worse still when passions bear the sway,
   Unbridled youth brooks no delay,
   He drives dull reason far away,
      With scorn avow'd;

" For *twenty* years she reigns at most ;
Labour and study pay the cost ;
Just to be rais'd is all our boast
    Above the crowd.

" Sickness then fills th' uneasy chair,
Sorrows press round with pain and care,
While faith just keeps us from despair,
    Wishing to die.

" Till the farce ends as it began,
Reason deserts the dying man,
And leaves t' encounter as he can
    Eternity."

LETTER.

        " *Blake's Hotel,*
    " *Thursday, Aug.* 21, 1817.

" My dear Mrs. ——— will kindly rejoice to see the old handwriting not shaken quite to pieces. Tell Mr. ——— that the wheat (and I passed through the principal corn counties) has a cold, lean look; not the rich, brown, glowing colour it used to wear in brighter seasons : 'tis become completely one of

‘ The pale, unripened beauties of the north.’

But, as people seem disposed to be contented, I will not croak; the hay is everywhere rotting on the ground; it will make good manure. Dear *Mr. Thrale* used to say when the 18th of August was at hand, every pond dry, every brook low, and all the hedges *white* with dust,— he would go to Brighthelmstone that he might *see water;* and now, every pond is over-flowing, every little brook become a river, and the meadows in flat grounds quite inundated. The best is, that the hedges are green as in spring; and—I know not how near we are to ruin, but buildings increase so that my knowledge of the town and its environs will hardly bring me through.——My dear friends will find *me* unaltered, and my nonsense of the old colour: a little giddiness in the head last night, was my worst complaint; a mere trifle, occasioned by the whirl; and I am better of it this morning.

" Meanwhile, if Wisdom *does* cry in the streets, as Solomon says she does, the horn-blowers drown her voice terribly. I wish to get my *work* done, and re-turn to a quieter region. Some part of that work will be unpleasant: I *must* go to *Streatham-park,* the wise folks tell me : poor, degraded, denuded *Streatham-park!*

E

It will be an odious day to me; but my hope is to finish *every* thing, and set my horses' heads homewards next Monday se'nnight. May I find dear No. 11, well and happy; comfort in possession, and pleasure in prospect! And may I, without repining, close my own views, so far as they relate to *this* world, rejoicing that, among many undeserved delights, I have enjoyed that of approving myself, dear Mrs. ———'s, &c.

" Most faithful and obliged,

" H. L. Piozzi."

Though it is not within the compass of my plan to transcribe all, or, possibly, the whole of *any* of her most agreeable letters, I could not resist the temptation of inserting the foregoing, which contains many characteristic traits worth preserving. What she says of the wet summer, and how sunny and dusty August *used* to be, is uttered in playfulness. She was eminently free from that common infirmity of age, the belief that all things and persons were deteriorated, and inferior to those of *her* day. On the contrary, her mind went on with the times; and she took pride, as I have often heard her declare, in believing that, on the whole, human intellect was advanced; and that morals, manners, taste and dress, were decidedly improved in these countries.

Above a year before the date of this letter, there was a sale by auction of the fine collection of portraits at *Streatham;* and *Mrs. Piozzi* took the trouble of writing out for me a complete list of the pictures, and the prices for which they sold. The following is a copy of the list she gave me ; it is different from one published about the same time in the London newspapers.

"THE STREATHAM PORTRAITS.

LORD SANDYS	£36	15	Lady Downshire ; his *Heir.*
LORD LYTTELTON	43	1	Mr. Lyttelton ; his son.
MRS. PIOZZI	. 81	18	S.Boddington, Esq. a rich merchant.
GOLDSMITH	. 133	7	Duke of Bedford.
SIR J. REYNOLDS	. 128	2	R. Sharp, Esq. M.P.
SIR R. CHAMBERS	84	0	Lady Chambers ; his widow.
DAVID GARRICK	. 183	15	Dr. Charles Burney, Greenwich.
BARETTI	. 31	10	Stewart, Esq. : I know not who.
DR. BURNEY	. 84	0	Dr.C. Burney of Greenwich his son.
EDMUND BURKE	. 252	0	R. Sharp, Esq., M.P.
DR. JOHNSON	. 378	0	Watson Taylor, Esq.,by whom,for

MR. MURPHY was offered £102 18s. but I bought it in.

This is a true account from the priced catalogue, with a thousand thanks for my sweetly-passed evening.—H. L. P.

E 2

I received the above from Mrs. P., March 24, 1817.
The sale took place in May, 1816: the portraits are
all painted by Sir Joshua Reynolds.

———

LETTER.—SLAVES IN ALGIERS, &c.

"Bath, Sept. 22, 1817.

" The bells are now ringing for the anniversary
of the coronation I so well remember enjoying the
sight of, from the Duke of Devonshire's box, Westminster Hall, fifty-five years ago. It would be curious
to speculate as to how many of those who assisted
that day in the procession, yet survive. Mr. Upham
has not at hand a set of the Annual Registers, or one
could have looked over the order of parade. The six
bridemaids are all gone before their mistress, who
must surely feel something of what I experience,
when seeing myself surrounded by all *strange faces!*

" Mr. ——— is come home from abroad; you remember ———. The D———s are returned too; and
make me laugh with their oddly expressed fears lest

he should write a book concerning the wonders he has
seen in Italy. One thing he told me would, however,
be pretty in a book, or out of it. He witnessed the
procession of catholic slaves liberated at Algiers by
Lord Exmouth; and felt, naturally enough, very ten-
derly affected. When they had carried their acknow-
ledgments to the foot of the high altar at St. Peter's,
and had heard mass with that grateful devotion which
distance and disuse contributed to increase, they returned, blessing our English people, who stood in two
long rows, outside the church door; and heard them
cry out, VIVAN I BRAVI INGLESI ! VIVA LA NOSTRA
SANTA RELIGIONE ! Oh, how I should have loved
those dear Italians ! . . .

"It would have been but a dull thing to leave
the world without visiting our great metropolis
once more, and seeing a capital city, which is
even now paving with *iron,* and lighting with *air!*
. . . . . I will not seal my letter without telling you
that Mrs. R—— has brought FOUR children at a birth
to her husband, who is seventy-two years old, and a
grandfather. . . . . . How did dear Mrs. —— like
my skin-and-bone country?"

Mr. *Upham*, mentioned in this letter, is generally known and highly respected in Bath and elsewhere. He was a great favourite with Mrs. Piozzi, who, in speaking of him to me, used to say that no man had half so many acquaintances as Mr. U.; yet numerous as they were, he had not, in moral worth, his superior among them, and rarely his equal in knowledge, or in the modesty which belongs to a man of real merit.

The queen (Charlotte) did not long outlive her *bridemaids;* though at the date of this letter she was in a tolerably good state of health; and, as it was reported, paid the compliment of a message of inquiry to the fruitful lady and her spouse, recorded by Mrs. P.

BRYNBELLA, &c.

" IT would be *too* cruel if you don't call at *Brynbella* coming back. I do wish Mr. —— to see the *fossil fish*, and the *Canalettis* we brought from Italy; and the old house of *Bachygraig*, celebrated by *Pennant*, and repaired by my dear *Mr. Piozzi* at a mon-

strous expense, because his little wife was vain of it.
I have been stung by a *dead wasp*, it seems! How
good you all were to keep the book out of my sight
so long! I read it by mere chance three or four days
ago. What pity that a man who knew so much as I
have heard this man did, when alive, should choose to
talk of what he knew nothing *at all* about,—my fortune and affairs!

" When *your* sect of honest men shall spring up,
we will not look among such as *Mr. Beloe* for
followers."

I had read, with mingled feelings of mortification
and disgust, what *Mr. Beloe's* posthumous publication
contained against her, and naturally avoided the subject in her hearing. Of what he has thought proper
to say, however, I shall here only observe that it is
scarcely possible to find in the pages of scandalous
literature, so great a quantity of malignity and mis-
representation in so small a compass, as the chapter
exhibits which the writer has devoted to reflections
on Mrs. Piozzi.

ALGIERS.

" I AM glad you liked W.'s account of the liberated slaves. It is touching; but candour must confess a respectful feeling for the Dey, who, as Mr. Finlayson informed me, showed all possible activity and courage during scenes he little expected to witness; exposing his person to the hottest fire ; holding up the *Koran* to encourage his troops; and when at last submission was found indispensable, *thus* qualified it by his interpreter :—' Look ye, gentlemen, God is God, and Mahomet is his prophet. We enter not into the counsels of the Most High! It is resolved, and I cannot now counteract it, that these men's punishment, most justly incurred, should at length, as it appears, find remission. All praise be to God, all honour to his prophet! To them alone I appeal for my conduct, and to them alone do I look for explication of this truly inscrutable decree.' I long to break prison, as much as the slaves did; but when I tell Doctor Gibbes that I take honey and take treacle, &c., he says, ' you must take another thing, *Mrs. Piozzi ;* you must take—*care.*' "

WALES.

" So you liked the scenery in my wild counties of *Merioneth*, and *Caernarvon?* It is very bold and very grand; and looking back upon those mountains from *Gwindie* in old *Mona*, *Mr. Piozzi* said, was finer than *Chamouny;* inasmuch as the ocean contributed to its superiority. You lost the *Suchnan*, however, pronounced gutturally; and you must go the *Penmanmaur* way back, if but to see that one odd sight, *my* favourite. * * * But here is not one word said yet concerning the Liverpool Lady, who reads printed books by the tips of her fingers; Miss Mc. Evoy: and discerns colours, though *stone blind*, and although a glass is put between her and them! I never heard such wonders; and well attested (as Autolycus's ballad of the fish—forty thousand fathoms above water) by seven justices, and a Doctor Bostock! Why *Carraboo* was nobody to this Miss Mc. Ivor, or Mc. Evoy,"

Miss Mc. Evoy was, it is presumed, one of those common cheats, who succeed with the ordinary world, because *no*-body could suppose that *any*-body could be so astonishingly impudent, &c. ! We help to delude our-

selves ; and that was the case in the affair of the female
rogue, *Carraboo*, to whom she alludes.   An almost incredible instance of knavery on one part, and *dupism*
on the other.   The pitiful jade who performed the
character of " *Carraboo, Princess* of *Javasu*," was an
infamous female of low condition, who passed herself
on the *Bath* and *Bristol* public for an Indian Princess,
&c., and when detected, which she speedily was,
proved to be a certain *Mary Baker*, who had been in
jail, and suffered whipping for theft.   Among the victims of the deceit she practised, was (but for a day
or two only) a Bath Physician, well known as a
gentleman of the greatest respectability and the most
humane disposition, and distinguished for scientific
attainments and general talents !   But there is sometimes a species of refinement in villany displayed
by *adepts*, by which it would be almost disgraceful *not*
to be deceived.

PRINCESS CHARLOTTE, THE QUEEN, &c.

" *Bath, Thursday, Nov.* 13, 1817.

" My dear Mrs. ———'s kind letter came in a happy
hour to disengage my thoughts from the current which
was carrying them away, and to restore them to their
proper channel, private friendship . . . . Poor
dear Lady S. will I fear be affected by this frightful
catastrophe of the Princess and her child. Every female
must feel not only afflicted but indignant, at one
express coming here after another, telling us all how
charmingly the business was going on. Forty-eight
hours of *agony!* But the *farce of life* must go on, till
death drops the curtain, I suppose.

" My heart feels assured that our *Mr. Soden* would
have saved the infant. When he and I meet, our talk
is of your family; our wishes all for your return. There
was a nice house too, six doors above mine, the field-
side of Gay-street, to be had the other day; but after
the Queen came, *nothing* was to be had. And Miss
———, who knows every body's actions and motives,
or thinks she does, tells me that Mr. ———'s brother

and his lady stopt at Worcester, because they could not hope for choice of abode here, while *Royalty* remained. Indeed *Bath* has been put to an enormous expense; and unless the Queen does come back on December 3d, as our inhabitants are taught to hope, they may well shut their shops, and mourn; for they will have just cause. My letter is full of mournful events, is it not? Yet, no black-edged paper! There is not a sheet to be purchased; and seven shillings were given for the *Courier* of Monday last, the 10th of November, *because* Jerome Buonaparte is mentioned as possessed of a distant hope, at least a *looking to* the throne of Great Britain!

" Colonel *Barry* is scarcely ever seen of late; and when seen, certainly looks ill."

This letter was received while myself and family were on a visit to relatives in Ireland, where we remained for some months; and thus escaped a winter of unexampled changes and tumults in Bath. But Mrs. Piozzi was constant in her friendly and entertaining communications; and always, as in the foregoing, touching on persons and occurrences of an interesting kind. Her admiration of *Mr. Soden,* the eminent surgeon, and her confidence in his great professional skill, were shared with many another. That the precaution which ever distinguishes the master in his art, might have preserved the unhappy young and royal lady, can scarcely be doubted: but— it is now too late to lament!

Colonel *Barry*, several years dead, was a general favourite, and our particular friend. In his day, he was admired as a man of superior talents, and extensive information; and his acquaintance cultivated by persons of both sexes, and in the foremost rank of society. That magnanimous soldier, and most amiable of men, the late Marquis of Hastings, with whom Colonel *Barry* had served in the American war, thought highly of him, and loved him as a brother.

The Colonel was a shrewd and sagacious observer of what was passing; and could see into the probable results of human conduct farther than most men. One instance of his penetration I will here mention. In the year 1812, I was sitting with him at his apartments in Orange Grove, Bath, when the very earliest intimation reached the public of *Napoleon's* projected expedition to Russia; when the

Colonel said, " that attempt will some how or other be his ruin: probably by his getting *too far* from his resources, and then the climate will destroy him." I wrote down this, as I thought, rather rash prediction, in Colonel B.'s presence, dated the memorandum, and said I should lay it by, and hereafter compare it with the event. What that proved, needs not be told!

BATH OCCURRENCES.

" Bath, Nov. 13, 1817.

" AFTER the tumultuous merriment, and the mournful depression which have succeeded one another in this delirious town, like the hot and cold fits of a tremendous fever, how refreshing is the letter of a true friend! .... Did not we use to agree that for folks in general, (not you and me), the fifth commandment ought to be changed to " honour thy son and thy daughter." Well! and so it ought. Poor old Mrs. ——, mother to the ——, lay dead in the house, which was illuminated with singular gaiety; while Mr. Webbe Weston, of the Crescent, whose daughter died a month ago in Italy, wrote under *his* front windows, " THIS IS THE HOUSE OF MOURNING." Two sombre black lamps just showed the words, half shaded by a black crape; and—never a vagabond in the town passed by, without respecting the signal of distress. Our Doctor Gibbes has had every honour paid him; yet I am not sure that your friendly notice of him in my letter, was less welcome than the eulogy printed in a Morning Post, which I never could get to see. He confesses . . . . . . , and also an account of the London theatres, the gas-lights, &c., which he describes eloquently to *me*. I took down the *first* book of Paradise Lost, and read him a similar description of *Pandemonium;* our *tête-à-tête* conversation so struck him that he put it into some paper; I forget what; all names suppressed, of course. *Apropos* to theatres; we have *Mr. Farren* here; nephew to *Lady Derby,* and *like* her. He played *young Mirabel* in *Farquhar's* " Inconstant," very elegantly, and with good spirit. — The mischief of distance is the not knowing what humour one's friends are in, and what impression is made on them by a tale of an occurrence which, two hundred miles off, seems of infinite impor-

tance! *This* town, I am persuaded, feels more than
any town, because—it was absurdly puffed up. " Hail,
Bath, the fortunate ! " " Hail, happy Bathonians ! "
written upon every wall, and lighted up in every gay
mode, as a transparency : such nonsense did I never
hear, such frenzy did I never witness ; and all extinguished in one little week, like the last day of
carnival at Venice ; and then Ash-Wednesday. A
Turk there (at Venice,) did say to some one who
repeated it ; " These Venetians have been *mad* these
last ten days, but the priest rubbed a powder on their
heads two mornings ago, (meaning the ashes,) and it
has really brought them to their wits again."

———

The above affords a very striking view of *Bath* at
a moment of extraordinary excitement. The royal
visit alluded to by Mrs. P. was undoubtedly designed
for the double purpose of producing pleasure to the
illustrious persons who projected it, and benefit to the
beauteous city in which they intended to sojourn.
The calamitous event which destroyed the hopes of
a people, converted the whole region into a scene of

disappointment and sorrow—almost, if not altogether, unexampled. Everything dismal, is, perhaps, more out of place in Bath, than it would be in any other town, or district of the empire. The passage in the first book of Paradise Lost, is surprisingly descriptive of the effect of " gas lighting."

> " From the arched roof
> Pendent by subtle magic, many a row
> Of starry lamps, and blazing cressets fed
> With *Naptha* and *Asphaltus*, yielded light
> As from a sky."
>
> Book i. verse 726.

And I believe she was the first person who noticed the lines of Milton, as prophetic of our modern brilliant invention. Her discernment assisted her to anticipate the deservedly high station in public esteem of Mr. Farren, as a comedian. When she made the remark contained in her letter, the critics, out of London, were not, as they now are, unanimous in his praise. She was, however, by no means such a judge of dramatic performers, as she would have been, with less good-nature, and more severity of character. But I have never known an individual so fond as she was of applauding the slightest pretension to merit of

F

any kind in others. She loved extravagantly to encourage the lowly and the timid; and could not recon-
cile herself to the act of finding fault. This disposition,
as may be supposed, disqualified her for the ungracious
duties of criticism; yet she could occasionally apply
the laws in such cases made and provided, with calm-
ness and discrimination; and was a most entertaining
companion in a theatre. I attended her one evening
in particular, to witness a performance of Kean's; and
was much amused by her remarks on that great but
unequal actor. Having asked her if he at all reminded
her of *Garrick*, her reply was favourable : she said—
" in some respects he does; he is for ever energetic
and often natural, which Garrick was *always ;* and then,
he is short and sprightly; and, like Garrick's, his little
frame seems constantly full of fire."

LETTER.—BATH GOSSIP.

" *Bath, Friday, Dec.* 12, 1817.

" My dear Mrs. ——— determines to be wise, grave,
and not write idle *flimflams* to her H. L. P. No

matter,—*I* shall send *you* a whole list. Flimflam the first; a curious story of the —— of —— (blanks make it still better) ; how she ordered a painter at Rome to paint her as the *Titian Venus!!* We must not say *dressed* in the character. It was cold weather, and the room necessarily heated by stoves. The man suffered cruelly from oppression of the lungs, lately injured by a violent cough; and going suddenly out into the frosty air, broke a blood vessel, and died.

" Flimflam the second.—How Mr. ———, the fine man here at Bath, sends daily presents to the Queen of England; trays of sweetmeats, and pastry made by his own cook; setting her Majesty's household to laugh at him !

" Flimflam the third, is a tale of a shopkeeper in Wade's Passage, running away with a woman of quality.

" Flimflam the fourth.—A steady assertion that there never was *any fortunate youth,* nor any Mr. ———; that no legacy was left, of any importance; but that the whole was a mere fabrication, to obtain credit for a swindler !

" What say you now to " *les on-dits* " of Bath ? . . .

Doctor G. does not forget his old friends; and is
sometimes so little of a courtier as to tell me slyly
what a pressing forward there is for notice in the
Pump Room; all eager to obtain attention for themselves or their progeny; all disappointed who cannot
succeed. The Queen visits Bristol to-day, and King's
Weston. It is heavenly weather for such a frolic!
And we all hear that her Majesty was enchanted with
Bailbrook. Her return was really a happy thing for
this town; but though well disposed (as it appears)
to gaiety, she has not yet visited the theatre, where
decorations of an expensive kind were prepared to
grace her appearance. Southey's "Maid of the Inn"
is got up as a melo-drama, and very interesting; but
plays are out of fashion; nothing they can do fills the
house. Have you read the "Welsh Mountaineers"?
It amused *me* of course. Good night! The sun sets
now almost behind your old habitation on Queen's
Parade; when turned about, how I shall watch its
passing Monmouth Hill, while lengthening days and
smiling skies will bring you safe home, I hope, to
your anxiously-expecting

"H. L. PIOZZI."

Much of this agreeable letter must, from distance
of time, &c., pass without comment on my part. I
think I have heard, but forget my authority, that the
lady who *sat* for the portrait of the *Titian Venus*, was
one of the sisters of Napoleon Buonaparte.

The story of " The Fortunate Youth," in *Flimflam*
the fourth, proved, not long after the date of her
letter, to be exactly as she had conjectured, a trick;
performed, with some success too, on the most generous and high-minded people on earth, and of
course the most easily deceived—I mean those who
are called the middle class in England; to whom,
as well as to the opulent and noble of the nation,
the tribute of praise and admiration is justly due
for a readiness to be charitable (as that word is understood), totally without example in other lands, either
in our own day, or in antiquity. What *governments*
do in other countries, is done by the *people* in Great
Britain. Perhaps it is not asserting too much to say,
that the voluntary contributions for the maintenance
of public establishments, and the relief of individuals
in adversity, in London alone, and in any given year,
exceed in amount the liberalities of the whole conti-

nent of Europe, in the same space of time.   It is to
be lamented that the generosity of *such* a people
should ever suffer by the arts of the impostor !

In one of her letters she says, " I have read with
pleasure the introductory pages to *Pamela ;* it would
not surprise me if I should be seduced to go on
through the whole work of our dear Richardson."

On the above passage I cannot help remarking that
her partiality to the writings of Richardson was, on
all occasions, proclaimed as here, and I believe it was
unqualified.   She used to say, she " loved Richardson's novels for *every* reason which can be assigned
as a ground of partiality."

They were associated in her mind with the persons
and occurrences of her early days; formed a constant
topic of conversation and admiration on the part of
Doctor Johnson; and had been studied and extolled
by many of the most enlightened and fastidious judges
of literature, and of moral and social interests, of the
age in which these splendid works first appeared.   It
therefore seems to me rather extraordinary, that *any*
one should now be found to treat Richardson's novels
not only as effusions to be derided for their imbecility,

but condemned as pernicious, and to arraign their author as a licentious writer. Yet a female, who, in the year 1824, published some *anecdotes*, &c., speaks thus of the works in question:—" People of common decency began to loathe Pamela." And of Clarissa she says, " the coffin and white satin were the license for its being still read: the brothel, and beastliness conducted to them, and therefore must be a fair way. Rousseau was decent compared to Richardson." And elsewhere this critical lady adds, "loose writers, among whom I do not scruple to number Richardson, notwithstanding all his sentimentality." In contrast with these sage and delicate observations, it may be worth while to recal the declared opinion of another person respecting Richardson, and to remember who that other was. Doctor Johnson, in a prefatory remark to the 97th number of "The Rambler," says of Richardson, that he is one " who has enlarged the knowledge of human nature, and taught the passions to move at the command of virtue." This number of " The Rambler " was written by Richardson, and in these words the moralist Johnson announces his gratitude, and describes his coadjutor.

LETTER.—THE QUEEN, &c.

" *Bath, Dec.* 12, 1817.

" I STILL see and *feel* that the absence of my friends
has made a long and ugly *parenthesis* in the last page
of *my* long, flat, folio life! We continue to make a
bustle here; that is, the people do who frequent the
court, and cluster round the queen wherever she goes,
as the buzzing subjects do about *their* queen bee.
We swarm too; for country folks come *in*, I am informed, every market day, for the purpose of seeing
her drink a glass of water. *La reine boit* used to be
a joke when Frenchmen said it, and now we say it
ourselves.

To-day she shows herself at Bristol, and would
have gone with two footmen only, had not sugges-
tions, wise ones I am sure, arisen from what Doctor
Gibbes (her physician) said,—of its being possible
her Majesty might be seriously incommoded in such
a populous city as Bristol.

Doctor G. is an admirable being; he has suffered
no distinctions to diminish his care for an old acquaintance!

Miss Mc Evoy is coming to Bath, to make us believe that she can tell who is in the room by feeling our shadows on the wall!

Pray, has our ecclesiastical history reached you? it is a very noisy one. The *barometer* fell in two hours from changeable to stormy, and so did the people's temper.

My ill fate forced me into the *Octagon*, when the Bishop of Gloucester preached for the Missionary Society. But, good Lord! how past all endurance was the heat! Think of the *squeeze*, and the scent of new black clothes! We sate, or stood fixed like seeds in a sun-flower; no room to thrust a pin between any two; the impossibility of escape adding terror to distress. I think the discourse was eloquent, but could not judge; my head was all amazed. Collections were not made at the door, otherwise Mr. Cruttenden, who made me go in with his family, said the society would have got 50*l.*, each paying only a shilling. But at the Guildhall, two days after, came the archdeacon, my friend Mr. Thomas, and entered his protest against the whole proceeding. He was hissed home by the Evangelicals, who followed him whooting (*sic*). The protest, however, is published; and Doctor Gibbes considers it as a beautiful composition.

Well, in the midst of these strange events, and fearful lookings to the future, Sir Francis Milman's (the physician's) son has written a tragedy; and they have applied to H. L. P. (as to a pert young hussy), for an epilogue. My *patron* was far away, so I could ask no counsel; but I hope you think I needed none for " rejection of such addresses." As nothing but kindness and good opinion, however, was expressed, my refusal was very gentle, though very steady : and I heartily wish him success. Adieu: do not let dearest Mrs. —— *believe* the flimflams I enclose: two out of the four, I fancy, are wholly false; but grave people *do* say them, and expect credit, which I cannot give.

Godwin's new romance pleases nobody : though I like the story of a man, who, early crossed in love, lives quite alone, treating his servants as mere automata, and only desiring to remain undisturbed: till—the fall of some planks discovers to him that an attorney, and his nephew, were settled in quiet possession of his spacious mansion, and ample domain;

and that his domestics were at the command of those men, assisting to keep him up as a confirmed lunatic."

———◆———

LETTER.—ROB ROY, FRANKENSTEIN, &c,

" *July*, 21, 1818.

" . . . . Make haste home, dear friends:

> " Still to my faults and follies blind,
> Oh come ; nor study for delays ;
> But keep the certain fact in mind—
> Of *short'ning* life, and *length'ning* days.

I last week kept my SEVENTY-EIGHTH birth-day : but, unlike other days and dinners, I felt fatigued when the company was gone. The sick Miss Allen, your next door neighbour in Queen's Parade, is at length *released*. Tell Mr. ——— that in Welch the word which means death, means likewise *enlargement* from prison: ANGHAD is the word. The ladies are all reading ROB ROY, long waited for, and, in my mind, good for little. 'Frankenstein' is a filthy thing ; and 'Mandeville' a dull one: they have their admirers, however."

In this brief extract there is a great cast of melancholy, yet something altogether singularly characteristic. She seems, by what she says, to have been employed in deep and solemn meditation on the *awful change* to which, at seventy-eight, she could not but know the near approach. But even in this frame of mind, books had not lost their charms for her. Her sentence on Rob Roy is severe; but she had read and reflected much; and she knew that mere popularity (often the result of newspaper puffing,) was no proof of merit in a work of any description. Rob Roy, she was aware, exhibited supreme talent; I have again and again heard her say so; yet she must also have been conscious that the book contains much vexatious prolixity, divers falsifications of facts, and grammatical solecisms; and not a few erroneous views of manners. This she must have seen, and indeed did see. But no one, whose opinion was worthy of attention, could be found more prompt than she was to applaud the (in her time *unknown*) author, for being what he unquestionably was, a man of genius; the test of which is, his having struck into unfrequented paths, and invented a new species of writing. In a great measure he surely

has done this; for the historical romances which were
the predecessors of the " Waverley " race, are of a
distinct class; as much so almost as the execrable
love stories commonly called novels.   Besides, it
should be for ever remembered to the honour of Sir
Walter Scott, that he, for many a year, delighted and
instructed the whole of, at least, the British world;
that he may be deemed nearly the most *popular*
writer that ever lived; yet in his twenty or thirty
thousand pages, cannot be convicted of having penned
one paragraph unfriendly to the interests of morals
and religion.

LETTER.—THEATRE, BOOKS, &c.

" Bath, Feby. 4. 1818.

" The weather has kept me within so long, I lose all
but the quite prominent stories of the times: for even
Miss W——has been snowed up for this long while;
and coaches cannot travel to the parties *any how.*   Mr.
Conway has had a flaming night of it, however.   I
dared not venture the crowd; but he must have gained

as much as Barry or Mrs. Cibber used to do, in my young days: the theatre is rather larger—is it not said to be—than old Drury Lane? But then they used to build the stage up with scaffolding, for favourites.

There is a new book come out since I wrote last; or did I mention it to you before? *Frankenstein.* His female readers are divided strangely; one girl told me she was so affected reading it alone, that she started up, and *rang* the bell from agitation of spirits. Another lady said, ' Lord bless me, what alarmed her, I wonder! it is a *rhodomontading* story; I *slept* over it.' But it is, as you observe, according to the frame one's mind is in. A petty shop-keeper in Westminster once related to me, how she went with many others to see the great Duchess of Northumberland's funeral; it took place at night, for the purpose of increasing the solemnity; and she was buried in Henry the Seventh's chapel. When at last one lamp alone was left burning on the tomb in that immense pile of gothic architecture, and the crowd was pushing to get out, Mrs. Gardner (that was her name) lost her shoe; and endeavouring to regain it, lost, as it were, the tide of company; and heard the great Abbey-doors close on her, with a sound that reverberated through all the aisles, precluding every possibility of making her case known to those without. 'Dear, dear! and what did you think, Mrs. Gardner, and what did you do?' 'Why, to be sure, Ma'am, I thought I should catch a shocking cold; so I wrapt two handkerchiefs round my head and throat; and crept into a seat in the choir, as they call it, where I fell fast asleep; not without a good deal of uneasiness, lest the 'prentice boy—since my poor husband's death—should lie a-bed in the morning, and shop should be neglected; till those sexton fellows, or whatever you call them, should let me get home to breakfast.' If ever I told you this 'round, unvarnished tale, before, the ladies will recollect it; but I think it is *not* among my *potted stories*."

LETTER.—FEMALE TEACHERS, &c.

" *Bath, March* 27, 1818

" NEXT to domestic occurrences, the public events now seize one's mind most forcibly: voyages to the North Pole, undertaken in a steam-boat; and a ship dug up in Africa, made wholly of *cedar ;* (there is a plank of it at the Admiralty, affording proofs of the fact :) besides, the Danish ambassador's assurances that an immense log of mahogany-wood, bearing the mark of instruments, was found the other day upon East Greenland, are things so new and strange, as must give pause to the wisest, and wonder to the boldest of those who are looking on with hope of seeing *more.* Bishop Watson's quarto volume of attractive egotism amused me whilst in reading; and I frequently stopped to reflect how odd it is, that people *talking* always of themselves should annoy those who will be entertained by their *writing* of themselves after death ! You may observe that his opinion of the intermediate state, coincided with that of Doctor Johnson : among the millions who know nothing of the matter, perhaps they knew *most.* I would much rather think with *Mr.* ———, and we are certainly left with permission to form our own conjectures.——I met your friend Mr. Falconer at George's on the Parade, one day; and we had such a *talk* about you, and he was *so* kind, that I grew not to be afraid of him at all, before the chat was ended.

Miss O'Neill shines away in her profession, we are told : and—the *Society of Instructresses* (at Clifton), can scarcely go any further, I fear, without setting people either to laugh, or be angry. They come into houses *unasked ;* run down to the kitchen, &c. ; inquire of the servants if their wicked and negligent masters do not keep them from the knowledge of evangelical truths ; tell them how wrong their ladies' conduct is ; and exhort them to attend such and such places of worship, in despite and defiance of authority so exerted ; then take their departure, leaving Bibles behind them. From whence, if they forbear to expunge the precepts of St. Paul, both to servants, and females in general, I think they leave condemnation of their own conduct : professing to *instruct* openly, and exciting dissention between the established ranks of life. It is, at best, a dangerous experiment, and the good resulting from it must be distant, if it ever arrives."

———

She had not seen Miss O'Neill when this letter was written ; but after we had both witnessed her performance, and conversed on that lady's claims to distinction, we agreed in thinking that she had considerable merit; but that her fame was the result of some circumstances not immediately connected with her talents, as a first-rate actress. Young and fair, she came forth at an hour when a dearth of eminent female performers prevailed : enthusiasm lent its aid, and she became renowned.

Speaking of Miss O'Neill one day, Mrs. Piozzi said, " she has a wonderful genius for *weeping ;* and weeping is *catching ;* and then people do not like to think they have been crying for nothing, and so it goes on ! "

As to the Society of INSTRUCTRESSES, it is to be hoped they have had their day. They meant well; enthusiasts always do; but seemed not to remember that good intentions will not ensure beneficial effects. Well-meaning persons of feeble intellects have perpetrated ten times more mischief in the world, than the wicked ones with sound understandings ; if the truly wicked ever have such.

LETTER.—THEATRE, BRAHAM, SIDDONS, &c.

" Bath, June 6, 1818.

" LONDON fashions render it impossible to go to a play: people are just coming out of Hyde Park as the curtain draws up; and the first course is scarcely over before the fifth act begins. So, Drury Lane shuts, I understand; and the Opera.

" We have got Mr. Braham; and shall get Miss O'Neill for a few nights: it will be pretty to compare her with dear Siddons; whose every accent, and action, in Belvidera, is familiar to my mind, and alive in my remembrance.

" Are you interested about the newly started up claimant to our Earldom of Huntingdon? The *moveables* have been long ago disposed of, we are informed; and such a man as the late Earl was, I have long despaired to see; and must not expect, from a youth bred in rugged life, as this nobleman has been. If the tale be true, no novel can compare with it for entertainment."

To draw a comparison between Miss O'Neill and Mrs. Siddons, would not be a task easily executed. There did not appear to me any other similitude between them than what arose from their sex, and their having devoted themselves to the representation of much the same cast of characters on the stage.

Miss O'Neill was neither tall nor majestic; and her face, which was nearly white, wanted force and variety of expression. She usually spoke in the same key, from the commencement to the conclusion of a passage; and though her action was frequently finely suited to the sentiment to which it was applied, yet she commonly permitted the requisite gesture, look, and movement to appear too late, and rather to follow than to announce what she had to say. She was also not unfrequently too deliberate in her utterance, so as to be on the verge of *drawling*, and to seem rather to recite than to personate.

Mrs. Siddons was, as to her person, in her youthful days, of lofty stature, and unusual grandeur of mien; and, though somewhat large of bone, was thin, and surprisingly graceful. Her countenance might, with strict justice, be called beautiful. It was composed

of the finest proportions imaginable; her mouth was
wonderfully expressive of good sense, sweetness, and
scorn. Her eyes were brilliant and piercing, and
could be seen to sparkle or glare at an incredible
distance on the stage; as all must recollect, who saw
her as *Lady Macbeth*, when she rose from her throne
at the solemn supper, and was descending to˙chide
her terrified husband. Or when, with swathed jaws,
and corpse-like aspect, she stalked in her sleep from
the back of the scene. The effect of her eyes was
greatly assisted by a power she had of moving her
eyebrows, and the muscles of her forehead. By her
countenance alone, she could signify anger, revenge,
sarcasm, sorrow, pride, and joy, so perfectly, that it
was impossible to misunderstand her, though she had
not spoken a word. She so constantly acted the character of great personages in affliction, that, on the
whole, she had a mournful visage, and an awful tone
of voice, very detrimental to the success of her comic
attempts; and indeed unfriendly to her efforts in the
less impassioned scenes of tragedy; or when she played
merely genteel women in middle life. At times, in
private company, she gave one a notion of a wicked,

unhappy *Queen*, rather than of a purely well-bred
gentlewoman.

When I made some such remarks as these to Mrs.
Piozzi, she said I was partly right; but that her
friend, Mrs. Siddons, could be infinitely comic when
she pleased, and was among her intimates; though
anything but a comedian on the boards. She then
added a very amusing description of her having, in
a family party, ordered the parlour-door to be made
fast, and proceeding to perform most of the part of
Sir Anthony Absolute, with astonishing spirit and
pleasantry.

When I speak of Mrs. Siddons, I refer to what I
knew of her more than five-and-forty years ago, when
she was a young woman, in the meridian of her fame,
and in all the bloom of her matchless endowments.

LETTER.—FRANKENSTEIN, &c.

" Bath, June 11, 1818.

" THE House of Peers is shortly to have an *Earl
of Huntingdon*, I am told ; and there is a remarkable

tale attached to the claimant's history, which calls
people's attention very forcibly; but perhaps it is all
Carraboo. For my own part, I feel attracted less and
less to the world I am quitting; and if some sudden
impression does touch my mind, there just remains
good sense enough to understand that 'tis a silly thing
to trouble one's head about the adventures related in
the *last inn* of so long a journey as mine has been;
and from such a distance, as the road appears, when
thinking of my early stages! No matter,—I have
lived to see the *kaleidoscope,* and a very pretty play-
thing it is; but those in London are of such brilliancy,
and such extent of combination, that ours make a
poor figure in comparison, I find.

" I see the Quarterly Review just brought in; the
articles are entertaining, as *Bills of Mortality;* an
old acquaintance is discovered, and we pause upon his
character! The first leaves cut by me shall be the
dissertation upon that horrid Frankenstein which I
teased you about. But I shall first make one other
trial, one other endeavour at thanking you for remembering me so good-naturedly, and with such tender
solicitude concerning my health. It cannot be better,

I believe, at my age, though often much worse than I wish it. When the crippled and exhausted and half-stupified poor creatures pass me in their wheel-chairs, decent reverence alone prevents my exclaiming with the Pharisee, ' God, I thank thee that I am not as others are,' &c.

" Now do write again soon, continuing for me that partiality which does so much honour, and, what is better, contributes so largely towards keeping *me* in tolerable humour with, dear sir, your ever obliged and faithful H. L. Piozzi."

————

When she wrote the foregoing, she was more than seventy-eight years of age; and probably such a letter altogether was never yet written by any one so old. The handwriting is most beautiful; while in the style, all the writer's original character appears in undiminished vivacity and vigour.

The story of the claims of Mr. Hans Hastings to the Earldom of Huntingdon seems to have greatly attracted her notice, and not without cause; it was actually the " romance of real life : " but the particulars are already before the public, and need not be

repeated here. The account given by Mr. Bell, the
barrister, who was chiefly instrumental in bringing
forward and establishing the pretensions of Lord H.,
forms a well-known and very entertaining volume.
With respect to Frankenstein, she explained to me
afterwards why she spoke of that work of genius and
fancy, as she did, and distinguished it by such harshness of epithet. Her explanation was, in fact, highly
complimentary to the author, for she confessed to me
that her objections were mostly founded on the circumstance of the vast power which the novel exercised
over her mind. She felt provoked on perceiving herself
fascinated by a fiction, so wild, so bold, and improbable. To the richness of the language and the sublime imagery which embellish the work, she did ample
justice.

Having intimated the likelihood of my memoranda
often proving desultory and unconnected, I need not
offer an apology for introducing here a remark omitted
in its place, on Mrs. Piozzi's mention of the name of
a gentleman in Bath, whom she does me the honour
to designate as my friend. Mr. Falconer is now
more correctly described as a physician, and the son

of the late Doctor F., than whom society did not possess an individual of greater respectability or more
various merits. He was in his time distinguished,
and is now remembered, in Bath especially, not only
for his extensive practice, but as a man of profound
erudition, of genuine, unostentatious benevolence, and
of the most unbending dignity of mind. This, which
is in no degree an exaggerated eulogy, will apply as
strictly to the learned and excellent man alluded to
by Mrs. P., and of whom she playfully says she
scarcely stood in awe. But she told the writer of
these notes, in speaking of the present Dr. F. one
day, that she could well understood how *any* one
might feel alarmed at the thought of being heedless in the presence of the purest moral rectitude,
information nearly unlimited, and discernment which
no foible could escape.

LETTER.—MISS O'NEILL, &c.

" *Bath, July* 6, 1818.

" THE thought of being so remembered, and so
cared for by ———, comes smiling to my heart, and

sets me off happily on my long journey. Shall I *try my powers* upon your brother at Worcester? If I go that way, I will. If nothing happens sooner to bring your family on my conversation carpet, as it is ever in my mind, a letter on my dressing table at Brynbella will at least console me.

"Miss O'Neill has fascinated all eyes; no wonder : she is *very* fair, very young, and innocent-looking; of gentlest manners in appearance certainly; and lady-like to an exactness of imitation. The voice and emphasis are not delightful to my old-fashioned ears : but all must feel that her action is quite appropriate. Where passionate love and melting tenderness are to be expressed, she carries criticism quite away. The scene with *Stukely* disappointed me : I hated to see indignation degenerate into shrewishness, and hear so lovely a creature *scold* the man in a harsh accent— such as *you now* are hearing in the street! My aristocratic prejudices, too, led me to think she under-dressed her characters; one is used to fancy an audience entitled to respect from all public performers; and *Belvidera's* plain black gown, and her fine hair twisted up, as the girls do for what they call

an *old cat's* card party, *pleased me not.* While—the
men admired even to ecstasy, as perfectly natural,
that which I believe delighted them chiefly—as it
was frequent and fashionable.

" What a brawling election this has been! *My*
best joke was correcting the motto worn on a flag
belonging to fourteen associated *tailors,* who went to
vote for some flourishing fellow, under canopy of the
words Liberty and Independence : I said let it be
Men and *Measures.* And now, if this never was
in a jest-book, it deserves to be there—does it not?
Among *les bon mots d'une octogenaire !*

"I leave Mrs. Holroyd surprisingly well indeed. She
often asks if I hear from you, and always sends love
and compliments—sincere ones—to your excellent
mother, (as she calls her), her valued friend."

———

There is a great share of point and solid meaning
in what she says of Miss O'Neill, and of her acting.
But her censure of the dress worn by that lady in
Belvidera, is misapplied.

Black is not only the colour generally preferred in
Venice; but of itself it tells a tale of sorrow; and

every one knows that much of sentiment may be conveyed by the hue,.as well as the form of raiment, on the boards. Besides, Jaffier's fallen fortunes would prohibit the slightest approach to *finery* on the part of his sympathising and afflicted wife.

Anything gaudy in her attire would appear to me infinitely more out of place, than even the meanest robe negligently thrown on.

Mrs. Holroyd was the friend of Gibbon, and the much loved sister of the late Lord Sheffield. She died several years since, at an advanced age; and was one of the most amiable of her sex. She possessed, with a temperament of great sensibility, the utmost suavity of disposition, the soundest possible understanding, and, as may be supposed from her rank in life, highly polished manners.

In her final illness, she was attended by Sir George Gibbes, who told me that her sweetness of disposition was unimpaired to the last; and her religious resignation such, that while he could scarcely refrain from tears, she smiled with hope, and said—" Dear Sir, I almost dread your professional efforts in my favour, for I *would* not recover, and long to flit away."

LETTER.—HELEN MARIA WILLIAMS, &c.

"Brynbella, June 18, 1818.

" My dearest Madam,

" Your obliging letter arrived yesterday. I am
but just come myself, making a slow journey
of it, and hoping to have seen something *like*
your husband at Worcester; but his brother and
family are residing in a beautiful cottage near Mal-
vern, and I could not resist sending him a *portrait* of
the place. The evening I meant to pass with *them* I
wasted in the china warehouse, but was delighted
that I could send you the *picture* of the house they
are inhabiting.

" Did I ever tell you of a Count Andriani, who dined
with Mr. Piozzi and me once in Hanover Square?
Helen Maria Williams met him, and whispered me,
before dinner, how handsome she thought him. He
was very showy-looking; and had made a long tour
about our British dominions. While the dessert was
upon the table, I asked him which was finest—Loch
Lomond or the Lake of Killarney? ' Oh, no comparison,' was his reply; ' the Irish lake is a body of

water worth looking at, even by those who, like you
and I, have lived on the banks of *Lago Maggiore*, that
much resembles, and little surpasses it; the Highland
beauty is a *cold beauty*, truly." Helen's Scotch blood
and national prejudice boiled over in the course of
this conversation; and when the ladies retired to the
drawing-room after dinner, ' I was mistaken in that
man's features,' said she ; ' he is not handsome at
all, when one looks more at him.' Comical enough,
was it not? Everything gets stupid this *hot* weather;
the very grasshoppers are silent; our large rivers,
Severn and Dee, creep dully and languidly along;
whilst the little trout-streams, once so sharp and
saucy, scarcely cover their slow eels, that keep close
to the bottom, hiding their heads in mud! Were
North-Wales people ever weary of *heat* before? It
is a new sensation to *that* native at least, who boasts
of yours and Mr. ——'s friendship; and whose feelings *to* the last, *at* the last, perhaps *after* the last in
this world, will be those of tender and grateful remembrance; so God bless you and yours, and send
you safe home to your affectionate and obedient servant. I am just going to see my curious old house,

which Mr. Beloe said dear Piozzi had pulled down.
The front gate bears his name, as having repaired
and beautified it."

———

There is in Sterne's searchings into the recesses of
the human heart, nothing better than what she here
records, in her anecdote of the ingenious Helen Maria
Williams; so rich a trait of character could not, and,
as appears, did not lie concealed from her penetration.

What she says of her visit to her old family mansion, and of the falsity respecting its being pulled
down, advanced by Mr. Beloe in his posthumous
volume, reminds me of a communication which Mrs.
Piozzi took the trouble to make to me, at almost our
last meeting.   It was to this effect,— that Mr. Piozzi,
with whom, she constantly assured me, every hour of
her life was happy, had, in compliment to her, gone to
very heavy expense in refitting the ancient edifice;
and that from a sense of grateful feeling to his memory, she always thought she could not do less than
accumulate every mark of distinction in her power on
his near relative, " And this," she added, "exclusively

of his own intrinsic worth, accounts sufficiently for my partiality to Sir John P. Salusbury;" of whom and his amiable lady, she was, with reason, exceedingly fond.

LETTER.—VALE OF LLWYDD, &c.

"Brynbella, 10th. Aug. 1818.

" OH, what a beautiful spot I am writing from ; the landscape so rich, the prospect so extensive, the sea so calm. I grieve we cannot enjoy the view together ; we are neither of us very *national,* yet certainly the scenery in both our countries must be preferred to that of England; except in particular districts. *France* is too little intersected to please my fancy ; the eye there is wearied before it has done being pleased.

" We are spoiling the sublimity of this vale of Llywdd; cultivating the fine heathy hills, lately so brown and solemn, like dressing old, black-robed judges up, in green coats and white waistcoats. Sir John S. has done better, and planted his mountains to a large extent, eighty acres, with fine forest timber. Many

H

friends think it a folly ; but *he* says, and *I* say, that, in
forty years, the wood will be worth as much as the
estate below.   And what signifies tearing men and
horses to pieces, to cultivate and manure these upper
regions, which will be more profitable when more in
character.   The *folly* was in forgetting to sow turnips
among the plantations, which they help to keep clean ;
and pay labourers besides.   Never was seen such a
harvest ; all our wheat will be in by to-morrow night,
and oats ready to cut on Monday morning.   But—
while corn is *ripening*, the people are *repining ;* a
spirit of discontent pervades every part of Europe, I
believe.   The labourers' wages at the Cross are twenty-
one shillings this day, for the week ; and when my
father lived at old *Bachygraig*,—the date of which is cut
in the weather-vane, 1537 ; the house which Mr. Beloe,
God forgive him, has said that dear Mr. Piozzi pulled
down,—they were only five shillings ; yet in those days,
I mean in 1740, or then about, all were well pleased
and happy, with their oat-bread and butter-milk ; nor
dreamed of wearing shoes, and eating roast meat,
except at Christmas and Easter.   Those who can
unriddle this enigma, are better financiers and deeper

politicians than I am. Besides that, these fine guinea o'week labourers will be treated with good bacon dinners every day. My father's hinds, as we called them, fed themselves out of their five shillings, and were happy, and their cottages clean, and the renters willing to keep a pointer for the squire besides. What a letter is this! exclaims dear Mrs.——from our H. L. P.! But *Solomon* says little can be expected from those "*whose talk is of bullocks;*" and I like to enter into the detail of this, my *first* and *last* place, well enough. Adieu, dear friends; for a short time, thank God! I wonder where at Bath you will *fix* your residence?

"My mansion is in the middle; and it was always *uphill home* from your house to that of, dear sir, yours ever, *H. L. Piozzi.*"

————

The author of this pleasant letter could not but admire the infinite loveliness of the vale from which she writes. She possessed indeed, in everything, the purest taste; the result, in all instances, of a perfectly sound understanding, acute faculties, and much know-

ledge; all of which are requisites towards the forma-
tion of *taste*. The preference which the coarse and
uninstructed give to objects disgusting to the man of
refinement, must seek some other name, for, *taste* it is
not. The Vale of *Llwydd* exhibits a multiplicity of
nearly matchless features in landscape; and may justly
be thought superior to many things of the kind in Swit-
zerland, and to any thing in Ireland; which, with the
exception of Killarney, and a portion of Wicklow, has
to boast of few spots worthy of a traveller's attention.
Woods are generally wanting; and the hovels in
which the forlorn natives are compelled to dwell, are
so foul, sordid, and vile in every respect, as, in con-
junction with the dismal apparitions of depressed
heart-broken peasants, crawling about in blue or black
rags, effect a painful contrast with the rich and smiling
verdure of their glens, and the peaceful, gently-swell-
ing hills blooming with heath, by which the *bits*
of natural beauty in Ireland are frequently, as it
were, framed in. Besides, the Irish rivers and moun-
tain streams have mostly a chocolate colour; and
the old and massive mansion and abbey of the
days of the *Edwards* and *Henrys;* the time-tinted

village church, with its mantle of ivy; the gigantic
remnants of the *Hall House,* or *Baronial Castle,* are
no where to be found.   There *are* castles, as they
are called; yet these are anything but picturesque;
being chiefly square, dingy, roofless towers, bare of
foliage, cracked, and tottering; usually of the age of
Elizabeth; standing in grim loneliness; and telling a
tale of past suspicion, political oppression, and military
tyranny.   Some such fragment was within view of
Charles Phillips, when he very sweetly apostrophised
O'Connor's fastness, and his well-beloved native land;
as the poet fancies it once to have been.

> " Isle of the fair, isle of the free,
> Isle of Love and Loyalty,
> This ruin'd pile is now—like thee."

The British peasantry, whose condition, one hundred years ago, Mrs. Piozzi seems to have thought
comparatively happy, could hardly have been, upon
the whole, even as good as it is now.   Their necessity
of toiling to live was not less; their luxuries were not
so numerous.   The social compact between man and

man, is better understood than it then was; and education is now more diffused. As to happiness, that must have been what it is at present: but little can be experienced by those who depend for employment and even existence on the will of others, and their own labour.

LETTER.—DROLL VERSES, &c.

" *Bath, Nov.* 1818.

" WITH a thousand thanks for the verses: they remind me of a Welchman's wit, about a century ago:—

Alma novem genuit celebres Rhedicina poetas ;
Bubb, Stubb, Grubb, Crabbe, Trapp, Young, Carey, Tickell,
    Evans.
Nine celebrated Poets soothe our mother with their song ;
Tickell and Evans, Carey, Trapp, Bubb, Stubb, Grubb, Crabbe
    and Young."

The original of this billet I had the gratification of presenting, some years since, to Doctor Sigmond, a physician well known in London, and distinguished for his general worth, the amenity of his manners, his taste, and talents. The Doctor had, at the time, entertained a wish to collect the autographs of celebrated persons; and was, I believe, pleased to possess a specimen such as the MS. afforded, not only of Mrs. Piozzi's sprightly turn of mind, but of handwriting, and that too of a lady in her seventy-ninth year, which has rarely been equalled. Of the Welsh Poet, I can give no account; and as to the translation, can only guess that it is hers.

THE PERSIANS; MRS. PIOZZI.

In the autumn of 1818, an invitation from Sir Geo. Gibbes, to " meet the *Persians* at dinner " at his house, led to the enjoyment of a very interesting and agreeable day. The foreigners alluded to, travelled in the train of the Persian Ambassador. One was a Median; the other a native of Persia; and both were men of rank, of various attainments, strong sense, finished manners, young, handsome, and cheerful.

They spoke English fluently; and presented themselves in their full, rich, eastern garb, with all the

quiet elegance of men of true consequence, habituated
to the world, and its refinements. Without speaking
too much, they carefully avoided the provoking vul-
garity of silence; and in their attentions to the females
present, they paid them that most flattering compliment to the sex, of undeviating respect, without
appearing to condescend. Mrs. Piozzi was of the
party, and told me afterwards that she had been
" intensely gratified." Remembering her really brilliant display of conversation ; the winning manners of
our host and his lady ; the wide intellectual field over
which we wandered; the lustre of lamp-light trickling
over the silver and china ornaments of the table; the
classic strangeness of the foreigners' raiments ; their
jet-black, bushy beards, sparkling eyes, and oriental
complexions; the result is a most entertaining
retrospect.

LETTER.

"*May* 29.

"DEAR SIR, this is how the Epigram stands in *my* book :—

> " ' Lumine Acon dextro, capta est Leonilla sinistro,
>   Et poterat formâ vincere uterque Deos.
> Blande puer! Lumen quod habes concede sorori,
>   Sic tu cæcus Amor, sic erit illa Venus.'

"Quære, would not the epigram have gained in value, had the mother and son been represented as each of them one-eyed? It would certainly have been more classical to have substituted the word PARENTI for SORORI; but I am never sure of my prosody. One could then have translated it thus :—

> Leonilla said—lend me that eye—to her son,
> Perceiving the boy, like herself, had but one ;
> For then we may manage the matter between us,
> And you'll be blind Cupid, whilst I shall be Venus.

"The writer of this epigram was Cornelius Amaltheus who printed a collection of poems at Amsterdam, in 1685. A protestant, I believe, though born in Italy ;

and who parodied in Latin verse, the catechism of the Council of Trent. But—who was it made the following epigram on a man eminent for his literature and conversation talents, but accused of drinking? Oh, I wish it had been—H. L. P. !

> Regnat nocte calix, volvuntur biblia mane ;
> Cum Phœbo Bacchus dividit imperium.

> If at evening we fear'd, what we never yet heard,
>   That our Phœbus to Bacchus would yield ;
> The morn's brilliant light, put such fancies to flight,
>   Showing Genius had won the fair field."

VERSES.

Soon after our meeting at this entertainment at Sir G. Gibbes's house, she composed the following lines, at such leisure moments as were allowed her while sitting in a private box in the Bath theatre. She sent a copy to the interesting strangers, and gave one to me.

" Mrs. Piozzi presents her best compliments to the Persian Noblemen, with good wishes for their safe arrival at home ; where

Each with a friend, or brother by his side
Shall feel the varying moments swiftly glide ;
  Breathe fragrant gales o'er fields of spice that blow,
And gather fruits unfading as they grow.'
There, on soft verdure negligently laid,
Beneath some high Palmetto's graceful shade,
Should European recollections rise,
And British beauties flit before your eyes ;
Let *Bath* be frequent in the pleasing dream,
Her fam'd physician, and salubrious stream ;
Nor wake, till pleasure calls, or power commands,
To soothe·your sovereign's care, or rule his distant lands."
" *Friday, December* 4, 1818."

LINES.

ON RECEIVING AN EMBROIDERED HANDKERCHIEF FROM ———, JANUARY 1, 1819.

  " What sweet remembrance find we here,
  From taste refin'd, and hearts sincere !
  Tho' fogs obscure the coming year,
  Your friendship still burns bright and clear :
  While thus my flutt'ring soul you cheer,
  And drive from age its nat'ral fear,
  I'll not think fortune in arrear,
  Or view with dread the distant *spear*,
  For who could feel that hour severe
  Which from such eyes can hope a tear.
                          " H. L. Piozzi."

It will be recollected that the writer of the above was, at the time of composing them, within a fortnight of being seventy-nine years of age. Her lines are in answer to the following, sent with the handkerchief.

> " Dear Madam, kindly condescend
> T' accept this trifle from a friend ;
> And in its candid aspect view
> An emblem of her love for you.
> Oh, may it never be applied
> To throbbing brow, or aching side ;
> Nor, witness heaven this wish sincere !
> Be rais'd to catch the falling tear.
> Were it endow'd with sense to see
> The splendour of its destiny,
> To feel that, being yours, it may
> Yet live in some immortal lay ;
> In story shine, and soar to fame,
> United with your deathless name ;
> Then might it look disdainful down
> On purple robe, or kingly crown."

LETTER.—ETYMOLOGY.

" *March* 15, 1819.

" THOSE who write the word *Satyr* with a Y, says Dacier, are of opinion with Hensius, Scaliger, and many more, that the Wood-Gods, Fawns, &c., gave

name to the poem: ' parceque les vers etant rudes,
nès sur le champ, et faits par un peuple encore
sauvage, et qui ne connoissoit d'autres maîtres que la
joye, et que les vapeurs du vin, ils etoient remplis de
railleries grossières, accompagnées de postures et de
danses, comme les paysans qui sautent lourdement, et
se raillent par des impromptus grossièrs.

> ' Fescennina per hunc inventa licentia morem
> Versibus alternis opprobria rustica fudit.'

" Now all this represents a Welsh Eistifoed exactly,
which is a sort of half-savage, half-satyrical game of
improvisation to the harp, and in use even at this
hour. The polished Casaubon, however, gave the
new reading, and said, with dear Mr. ——, that the
word *satyrus* could never have made *satyra*, but *saty-
rica;* and the etymology must therefore be drawn
from *satur*, making *satura* and *satira*, in allusion to
the fulness (*satiety*, I suppose,) of *Ceres's salad;* for
they presented at her games ' un bassin de toutes
sortes de premices;' and this custom was not unknown to the Greeks; among whom, however, satires
were unfashionable. Though I know not what else

to call the chit-chat dialogue of Theocritus laughing at Sicilian *gossipry*.

"And now forgive this intrusive foolery, from poor, old, superannuated, No. 8, Gay Street."

———

LETTER.—WESTON SUPER MARE DESCRIBED.

"*Weston Super Mare, Sunday, July* 11, 1819.

"In the hope that my dear friends have so far conquered their difficulties, as to like a little change in the course of their ideas, I sit down, overagainst the North-American coast, to tell them in what an odd place I have *located* myself, using the phrase of Cumberland, everything pleasant without, everything most wretched within. Doctor Johnson would have said that the negative catalogue of comforts in this place was of an immeasurable length indeed. No chairs, no tables, not a chest of drawers, or bureau, as we call it, in the town. No newspaper later than the 3rd of July; they put one of the 1st into poor Mr. G.'s hand, who pays five guineas per week for a house resembling a habitation in Savoy; yet his lady gives tea-parties,

and asked me; but my soul disdains it. I live at the
hotel, have a good room to sit in, a clean bed to sleep
in, asses' milk to drink in the morning, and more food
than all my family can consume, for ten pounds a-week;
and we are a man, three maids, a baby, and myself; so
I am best off. Not a book in the place, but one Bible
and one Paradise Lost; I have got *them,* so am best off
again. But Cocker's Arithmetic would be as great a
wonder here, as Johnson's present of it was to the wench
in the Hebrides. Necessary enough, though; for if you
purchase a phial of tincture of myrrh for your mouth,
they make you pay double price, because you took it
without *asking advice* of the medical man in the town!
Now for the *per contra,* as we commercial folks say.
The sea has every beauty; islets, like St. Helena in
miniature, or my own country; St. Tudwell's full in
sight, and good bathing machines; the tides magni-
ficently high; and a constant storm, at least ever
since my arrival; the roar of which, close to my window, lulls me to better sleep than I have enjoyed for
a long time. And when you direct your looks down
the Channel, I am told, *Newfoundland* is the nearest
point they could repose upon, if strengthened, like

Adam's, in the last book of the only volume our place possesses.

" This is Sunday, and we have only prayers; those prayers only in the afternoon; while the population is prodigious, and people flocking hither from the interior of the country, by way of enjoying our very, *very* sweet air, and fine view. How is *Edward?* quite well, and the very best boy in England, I trust. To divert himself at two years old with a pencil, is exceedingly beyond the power of other children;— young Bertie Greatheed, and Sir Thomas Lawrence, were the earliest artists I ever knew. And now, dear Sir, when you have a leisure hour, tell me what the world is saying and doing. This little nook never sees anything but a donkey-cart, or a sick lady mounted on poor Dapple; and regiments of what I call *infantry*, under seven years old."

———

Something momentous to parents, and superintendents of youth in general, may be gathered from what she says of an early display of talent. True genius is rare; and most rare is such as was possessed by

Lawrence; who, in fact, owed so much to nature, and so little to instruction, as to excite a doubt as to the necessity of teaching; which can do nothing for the stupid, and not much for plodding assiduity, and half-talent.

Parents would do well to shun an error into which they are but too apt to fall;—that of mistaking inclination for ability; and may rely on it that though very clever children should be assisted by masters to the utmost, very clever children are rarities; and that the hours of their offspring, and their own money, might be much better employed, than in striving to convert *mediocrity* into *greatness*. The process is, in most cases, like teaching a bear to dance; it is very well, when done, for a *bear*, but after all, very bad dancing.

LETTER.—ANECDOTE, &c.

" Weston Super Mare, July 18, 1819.

"A POMPOUS man—a Mr. Ray—I was once acquainted with, discovered some seditious tracts to have been written on French paper, by means not unlike those you mention, thirty or thirty-two years ago. I

I

have probably told *you*, who know all my stories, how, when he was named a *Prothonotary* of some law-court, an humble friend came cringing with, ' Sir, I wish you joy, Sir.' Seeing his patron stand as if fixed against the wall, ' Sir, I beg pardon, Sir; but I thought it was proper for me to say, Sir, how glad I was that you are become a thermometer.'

" Anacreon Moore is got into some scrape, is not he? He will want a *Mr. Ray* to help him out. My newspaper, the only one in this place, tells me nothing but the Ladies' dresses who went to Carlton House, in costumes of different courts ; curious enough ; but they who want to quarrel, will quarrel about *that.* Is the Duke of Kent's daughter baptized by the name of *Charlotte,* or is she *Alexandrina Victoria?* Nobody here can tell; but everybody can blame those who gave the poor baby names which no one can speak, or say he has ever heard of.

" We have heavenly weather; and a *cool* comet that serves to amuse, but cannot much alarm us. The sea beautifully broken by two St. Helena-looking rocks, which we call the *Holmes;* and good savage bathing among stones and pebbles; poor machines, which donkeys cannot draw in or out; and horses I see none; young salmon not a quarter grown, and miniature soles about as long as *your* hand; none longer: infants innumerable for the benefit of salt water dips, which they abhor most religiously:—and *old* stories which one has heard forty times told. Our place of meeting is at the hotel-door, where we ask how Weston agrees, and whether the air is not particularly sweet here? I somehow fancy it *is*. My fellow-lodgers have been diverted by an April-fool trick out of season, played me by young S. Six days ago here comes a poor man, a labourer, in a smock frock, inquiring for Mrs. Piozzi. See her he could not; for one eye was quite out, and the other nearly extinct: hear what she would say to him,—impossible; he was stone deaf. But he could tell my *Bessy* in *Welsh*, how he had begged *Sir John* of *Brynbella*, as he called him, to give him two pounds, *because* his honour's good aunt used always to give him two pounds on a Whit-Sunday morn. *Bessy* believes that he plagued S. so, that he was at last provoked to say,—' Well, go look for my good aunt; you will find her at Bath.' The wretched man took him *au pied de lettre*, and walked all the way, till hither he came

for two pounds, sans eyes, sans ears, sans language,—
or good health.

" When we had cooled his fever, I despatched him
across the Channel here, into the Principality; where
he will do, at least better than in England; having
lain in the *street* at Bath, the night before we saw him.
A good supper was, however, likely to have comforted
him; but this was a hotel, a cut-finger club; and
some one who *had* eyes, snatched his plate from before
him who had none, and left him to the lamentation
and derision of our fellow-lodgers and boarders. Such
is the world, and such are its inhabitants."

———

I am unable to recall to memory in what species of
troubles the celebrated translator of Anacreon was
involved, at the date of Mrs. Piozzi's letter. Probably
nothing very formidable, or the world would have
enlarged on a subject connected, in the smallest
degree, with one so important in the sphere of genius
and literature, as Mr. Moore; who, equally a master
in prose and verse, holds even a higher place in public
estimation, and in this age of superior refinement,

than did Pope in *his* day ; and who, as patriot and
poet, will be known to nations which are yet to be.
Her opinion of Moore as a literary character, and a
man of general talents, was the same as that of
millions who are familiar with his name; but she was
not, I believe, acquainted with the bard; though the
humble writer of this can boast of being so; as well
as of being his fellow-townsman; and gladly takes
the present opportunity of saying, that a person of
such variety of claims to the love of his intimates,
and the admiration of his country, has rarely existed.

LETTER.—MRS. SIDDONS, &c.

" Weston Super Mare. Sunday, 25*th July,* 1819.

" NOT so the few people I converse with : ' they
apprehend nothing but jollity,' like pretty *Perdita*
in the *Winter's Tale.* A lady twice *her* age, told me
this morning that the people were choosing a new
parliament, and that the ladies would be admitted to
hear *their* debates. ' The old fashioned churls shut
us out,' added she, ' but we will have some *fun* now.'

Surely the Gulls, and the *Gulls' horn-book* would be
more companionable than such *charmers.* No one
will believe the nation in danger: poor old Britannia!
surrounded with fire as she is, till, like famous Madame
de Blanchard, we see her tumbling from her proud
height at once : and then the French will cry ' Ah,
mes amis ! quel beau coup de theatre.' Dear Siddons
thinks only of her own glory, 'tis plain; and nothing
can fill a mind, not quite preoccupied, so full as her
reading of *Macbeth.* True does the *Courier* say, she
acts the ghost-scene in that play better than Garrick
did. *He* bullied the spectre, and appeared to call
him names; as, with more propriety, *Satan* treats
Death in Milton's poem. Mrs. Siddons, when she has
said ' hence ! ' recoils into herself, and adds, in a low
and terrified tone, ' horrible shadow !' then recovering,
cries out triumphantly—' unreal, mockery—hence ! '
And wisely did Doctor Johnson say that history
was a magnifying glass; ' for when you read' were
his words, ' that Rome or Athens was in consterna-
tion, not a creature was *consternated ;* some went to
work, others to see the play; and no man ate less
supper, for all the proscriptions of Cæsar, Antony, and

Lepidus.' In the year 1780, however, he changed his note; as witness his letters to me, where he confesses that everybody *was consternated*. My astonishment is, perhaps, greater, that the people of our Stock-Exchange at London, should suffer themselves to be baffled, or swindled out of near a million of money, by *babies ;* boys of fourteen and fifteen years old, who made themselves *bears*, the papers say, they ought to be styled *cubs*, for no less than £ 900,000. Hannah More has written a new book, and the name has slipt my memory. Sam Lysons's death displeases me; he picked up such *odd things*. Indeed, I remember many years ago, when we breakfasted with him at his chambers, that he showed me a *snug corner*, as he called it, of his library; and told me it was full of all the caricatures, and insolent speeches made on my marriage with Mr. Piozzi! I wonder if he burned them? If he did not, I trust his brother, the clergyman, will; for he is a man with a family, and will not see any *fun* in making enemies. Adieu, dear sir, and accept the kindest wishes of your *oldest*, perhaps *newest* friend, that is as affectionate as your poor

"H. L. P."

In this letter she alludes to the strange and horrible fate which had recently overtaken Madame Blanchard. As soon as it was perfectly dark, she had ascended in a balloon, from, I think, the gardens of *Tivoli* in Paris; lights were attached to the machine; and when at a great height in the air, and while the multitudes in the grounds from which she rose, and throughout the whole city, to which she was visible, were shouting in admiration of the spectacle above their heads, the balloon caught fire, and she dropped screaming to the earth. It is needless to add, that she was destroyed: but one cannot help imagining what may have been the direful sensations of the hapless woman, when falling in flames from the clouds of night, hurrying to inevitable death, and—for the *last* time—hearing the human voice, ascending in cries of terror and despair from the crowds below. The power of *thought* is immense; and, short as were the moments allowed her for thinking, we feel that she *must* have thought; but what, and how much, no force of imagination can conceive.

Her observation on Mrs. Siddons' manner of acting the ghost-scene in *Macbeth*, is undoubtedly just criticism. How Garrick managed the passage in question, she more than insinuates ; but if it was as she states, he misconceived the fine sense of the poet, or rather lost sight of it altogether. There is much more of vigour and beauty of conception, in supposing the words "horrible shadow," to be the low murmuring of terror, than that they should be delivered as loud, personal objurgation.

The words which follow, " unreal mockery," are, in Mrs. Piozzi's manuscript, not separated by a comma, as I have written them, and as being distinct epithets, but as one compound; and probably so they should. There is something in the modern reading and punctuation too precise for Shakspeare. " Unreal mockery" is no more an impropriety than the old and authorised phrase, " *false traitor.*"

I believe the title of Mrs. H. More's publication, in 1819, was " Practical Piety."

Mr. S. Lysons seems to have been one of a class of persons, not so uncommon as they are provoking, who, from a baboon-like disposition, and a total want of correct feelings, not through absolute depravity of heart, derive pleasure from the act of making the sensitive and delicate writhe with anguish!

———

LETTER.—SEBASTIAN CABOT, &c.

" Dear Mr. ——'s saying that the further from Bath he found himself, it was the further from comfort, gives me persuasion he is returned by now to scenes of social life. I could not have believed *any* place in our island so removed from them as I find poor *Weston Super Mare.* When I offered the principal house here a draft on Hammersley and Co. for £50, ' Ay, sure,' was the reply; ' but who is Mr. Hammersley? does he live at Bath, or Bristol?' *He* would have been but little flattered by the inquiry! Do they not tell some story of a lady, who, thinking she should make court to the great *Linnæus,* said, ' Ah! dear Sir, I believe your name is known all over Upsal;' Upsala, as they call it.

" With regard to names, can you tell me why we call these little islets here the *Holmes?* Steep

Holmes, Long Holmes, Flat Holmes. It is a Saxon word, of course. *Holme-don*, indeed, seems Scotch:—

'Oh Douglas! Hadst thou fought at Holmedon thus,
I ne'er had triumphed o'er a Scot,'

says Hotspur; but these pretty, little, odd places, on one of which there is a brilliant lighthouse, lighted with gas, do not,

'Like rich and various gems, inlay
The unadorned bosom of the deep,'

but afford short pasture for a few *muttons*, and shelter for rabbits innumerable.

"South Wales lies so temptingly near, that many people go thither *a pleasuring*; James, our man-servant, among others. That evening, however, a marine vapour, uncommon, excepting when the atmosphere is preternaturally heated, suddenly arose, and took all sight from our pleasure-seeking party, even the sight of their own danger. *Au reste*, as the French say, no danger threatens *us* here, either from thundering clouds, or fiery reformers. A soft and balmy, though a bracing air, blows constantly but mildly from the

sea; and here it certainly *was* that Sebastian Cabot
stood on the shore, where my little wretched house is
built, and, looking down the Channel, planned his dis-
covering voyage to North America, about Newfoundland—the first that salutes adventurers who turn
neither to right hand nor left, for sixteen or seventeen
days.   He was a Venetian pilot, you remember, and
having brought a little trading vessel safe to Bristol,
stayed there for twenty years, during which time
Weston Super Mare was his favourite excursion; and
they have preserved his memory in a picture that
hangs in the Town Hall, Bristol.

" I picked up much of this conjectural intelligence,
and tolerably intelligent conjecture too, from a coarse
man who lives here, I believe.   But there is much
lost by being fastidiously resolved to converse with
none but *conversers*.   When dear Siddons lived much
at my house, I used to blame *her* for too much delicacy, and said that it was

' Wisdom at one entrance quite shut out ;'

but she could not accommodate herself to rough in-
structors.   Apropos to Siddons, I fancy she never

read the lines you mention, without recurring to old usages. After Churchill's ' Rosciad,' Mrs. Pritchard's mode of acting *Lady Macbeth* was looked up to as a model; and I have heard her great successor in the part profess repeatedly to have had very powerful prejudices to contend with, concerning the night-scene; and whether these good old usages would permit her to take the candle in her own hand; which, however, she persisted in till approbation followed. But, if *your* mode of reciting the lines, ' when she to murder whets the tim'rous thane,' ever crossed her mind, I question her daring to introduce it; and the *reading* would have afforded her the best time to try.

" She read the scene between *Malcolm* and *Macduff*, so as to break all our hearts; indeed her power of amusing five hundred persons without any additional help, was to me a greater proof of superiority over common mortals, than any acting of one, or of ten characters could bestow. I am here a person of much importance; nobody has a newspaper, nobody has a smelling-bottle but myself; so I lend them about, and look consequential. ' Lord Cowper is a great man here,' said one, ' because 'tis *Florence*, and he is not

known.' ' Why does he not live at *Prato* then,' said
Jack Ramsay, a boy about twelve years old; ' he
would be a greater man still!' "

———

Why the *Holmes* are so called, is not quite clear,
Holmes, in the Saxon, mean hills, the bottoms of
which are rendered fenny by rivulets.

Mrs. Piozzi was, I presume, not thoroughly informed as to Sebastian Cabôt; his father, whose name
was *John*, it is said was a foreigner settled in Bristol;
but *Sebastian* himself is claimed as a native of that
ancient and opulent city, where he is stated to have
been born about 1477.

I have forgotten to what she refers in her remark
on the night-scene in " Macbeth:" possibly to something said by me as to the action which, as I conceive
the poet's meaning to have been, ought to accompany
the delivery of the words —

    " But screw your courage to the *sticking* place," &c.

When the manner of *sticking* or planting a poniard
should be imitated. And this reminds me, that we
once conversed much on the subject of the manner

in which Mrs. Siddons sought for the taper, in the
scene in which *Lady M.* walks in her sleep; when
Mrs. P. seemed to think her right; which, I confess,
I did not. The great actress used, as it were, to *feel*
for the light; that is, while stalking backwards, and
keeping her eyes glaring on the house: whereas, I
have somewhere read, or heard, that the somnambulist
appears to look steadily at the object in contemplation,
and, in fact, sees it distinctly. It never was my chance
to encounter any one walking in sleep; and very few
have beheld such an exhibition; but an ingenious
friend of mine, and intimate with Mrs. Siddons, told
me that *she* once did witness the fact; and if so, in all
likelihood took her lesson for the splendid scene in
question from nature.

In her *reading* of the play, we may easily suppose,
from her fine native understanding, and matchless
power of expression, that she must have given the
dialogue between *Macduff* and *Malcolm* with wondrous effect.

Though we frequently met subsequently to the
date of the letter last transcribed, I do not recollect
that Mrs. P. told me who young Ramsay was, whom

she mentions as being at Florence; but the name recalls one of her narratives of a Mrs. Ramsay, an acquaintance of hers: and, I believe she said, the wife of an artist. I happened to speak of a collection of Scottish songs, known by the title of Allan Ramsay's Lyrics, but in which the author of " the Gentle Shepherd" had no concern. It had, I told her, as I was informed, its origin in the accident of some young men of talent meeting in Edinburgh at a tavern kept by one *Allan Ramsay*, and amusing themselves by producing, from time to time, their best attempts at lyric poetry, for the entertainment and criticism of each other. These effusions were at length arranged and published in the name of their Landlord; but have often since been received as the work of the Scottish Theocritus. She said that for her part she had a suspicion that the " Gentle Shepherd" was written by a person of the name of Thomson; but that, somehow, there was a sort of fatality attending all people called *Ramsay*. " Your story," she observed, " is new to me; and now I, in my turn, will tell you a *Ramsay* history of a very different kind." She then related what follows; and which may as well be introduced into this portion of my *Piozziana*, as elsewhere; though in no way appertaining to anything in her letter, except to this same name of *Ramsay*. " A Mrs. Ramsay, whom I well knew, was a most extraordinary, steady-minded, and gentle-mannered woman, as my tale will show. She was extremely ill at night; and calling her confidential maid-servant to her bed-side, whispered her— ' Jane, I am dying; but make no noise, because if you do you will wake Mr. R. (then sleeping soundly in the same room); and you know when his slumbers are broken he grows nervous, and cannot fall asleep again; but come you in the morning at the usual time, when I shall be dead, and he will have had his full allowance of rest.' And so saying, died accordingly." This anecdote cannot be fairly matched by any I have to tell. But the transaction nearest to it in point of *sang froid,* and attention to the feelings of others, on my records, is what, as I have somewhere read, took place between a certain French prince, and a nobleman of his court, to whom the former paid a farewell visit, when the other was at his last gasp. But though his lordship's breath was almost gone, his politeness was not: as his address to the royal visitant will witness: "I am penetrated, your Highness, with a deep sense of the honour this visit confers on me; but—I am at the point of death, and trust you will forgive me if I should find myself forced to make a few hideous and unseemly grimaces in your august presence."

LETTER.—FEMALE CRICKET-PLAYERS, &c.

"*Weston Super Mare,* 25*th Aug.* 1819.

THE *times* do exhibit a frightful foreground, a black and cloudy offskip: figures dancing *à la ronde,* and Folly jingling her bells to put them more and more out. The odd persuasion which men encourage to blind their own eyes, is to me one of the proofs of real danger; the present is a mere consequence of the past, and presage of the future. Female *cricketers* make room for female *Reformers,* who will give place to *Poissardes;* and a bad day it will be for quiet folks, when assassination becomes a duty. Mrs. Adams's handsome daughter, since dead, told me that she asked a *pet* labourer in their pretty garden near

Dublin, if *he,* too, would join the rebels? 'I don't
know, Miss,' replied the fellow; 'they have *sworn*
me.'—'Oh! but dear Andrew, sure *you* would not
kill mamma, or me! what is it they have done to you,
Andrew?'—'Why, Miss, they say I'm a *Lieutenant,*
but I am only a poor man, as I was afore.' And yet
this very fellow did betray the family; and the ladies
were within half an hour of death; but that Sir John
Moore came galloping into Wexford, with two or
three officers, and a handful of men, crying 'King
George and the army for ever!' and away scampered
the reformers, throwing themselves into the very river
for fear. We shall go on, I dare say, to see worse,
perhaps. I have a next-door neighbour here, a
superannuated beauty, who is all of my mind; nor
could I empty my head of a strong resemblance she
bore to some one lying back in my memory: till at
length, hearing some of her family call one another
B——, I asked her if she could forgive my freedom
in inquiring whether there was any relationship
between her and the handsome actor of that name,
first husband to Mrs. K. 'Madam,' was the reply,
'poor William was my brother.' Now, praise my

power of recollection; I never saw that man in my
life but twice : once in *Prince Hal,* and once in *Jaffier.*
Conway's acting the first of those characters brought
him back to my mind; but B.'s beauty was all in
countenance; not a towering figure and graceful
person like Conway, but with a face of semi-celestial
expression. And he was not my cousin; but his
father, Owen Salusbury B., wore my name, and I feel
quite an interest in this sick lady, whose resemblance
to her brother must be very strong; and she says they
were reckoned like.

"Cabôt and Columbus were very ill used indeed; and
America, named after that flourishing fellow Vespucius,
seems now in no good way, N. or S. Doctor Johnson's odd remark on the Hebridean Island, bears such
perfect testimony of its truth, one cannot doubt it an
instant; and how comical it is with its grave reference
to the velocity of light.

"I mean to come home to Bath as my last residence
in this world. It is the best place, as you kindly
observe, for me; the safest and quietest : and I shall
lay my life down among friends of God's giving, or my
own making—as we please to term it; but they are

bestowed by *him*, call it how we will. Till then, and ever, I will call myself, dear Mr. and Mrs.——'s *obliged,* and grateful, and faithful   " H. L. P."

———

She seems, in the above letter, to have taken a rather gloomy view of the condition of public affairs at home. But she saw deeply into every object of her contemplation, and especially into human nature, which she knew to be for ever the same.

The state of the general mind cannot be over healthy, where those things happen to which our lamented and amiable correspondent alludes. There *is* something preposterous, not to say gross, in women playing *cricket;* it being, indeed, what no female can do, unless badly. And were it possible that she could excel, or equal any expert male player of that athletic game, her superiority would have an effect as ridiculous and unnatural as what would be produced by seeing a boatswain, or life-guardsman, executing needle-work behind a milliner's counter.

On the like principle, female *Reformers* are out of their place. A distinguished nobleman, writing to his relative on the subject of the clerical dress, says

that a parson ought not to assume an air of fashion or
finery in his attire, because he can be at best but *half
a beau !* A lady lies under much the same disability
with respect to political topics : she can, at most, be
but half a *politician ;* and had much better not be
any thing of the kind.

The story of Andrew, the gardener and rebel, may
be strictly true. With the labouring classes in Ireland, an oath is a most sacred obligation. A country
fellow there may be persuaded to take an oath to do
almost any thing. For instance, to abstain from
drinking to excess, to kill a benefactor, &c. ; and
should he make this solemn vow, he will keep it;
though, to be intoxicated, and to evince his gratitude
for kindness received, are decidedly among his darling
pleasures. This disposition to feel the sanctity of a
covenant with heaven, might, I suspect, be rendered
instrumental in conferring boundless benefits on himself
and on his goodly country. Some such beneficial consequence might possibly arise, were the members of the
Romish priesthood judiciously and liberally counte-
nanced. I speak from long and familiar acquaintance
with the village clergy of the Roman Catholic per-

suasion, when I say, that no man in any supposable
situation in civilised Europe, from a monarch to the
meanest land proprietor, has such powerful influence
in the circle in which he moves, as an Irish Parish
Priest. And I fearlessly add that, generally speaking,
he is the most laboriously, the most usefully, and the
most benevolently occupied individual in society.
This would be proved by a slight survey of some of
the duties he is required to perform. He is compelled,
by his calling, to dwell among the naked, the hungry,
and the despairing. However tender may be his
heart, his own means are scanty, and he is obliged to
witness woes which, in a worldly sense, he cannot
mitigate; and only can soften to the sufferer, by bid-
ding him not to expect any thing in this life but a
continuation of wretchedness; and that his hope must
be in what he beautifully calls " *the meadows of ease*,"
hereafter. That submission, not amelioration, is his
portion: that he must accept of penitence and prayer
in lieu of food and raiment; that he must toil on; still
drink of the waters of bitterness; and do all this without a murmur! The man who fills this part, and
likewise contrives to be confided in as a friend,

respected as an adviser, and loved as a parent, (and there are few catholic priests of whom more might not be said,) were he duly encouraged and assisted by government, could surely be made to operate most importantly upon the national character.

———

LETTER.—THE BISHOP OF MEATH.

"*Weston Super Mare, Aug.* 29, 1819.

. . . " WHAT sweet weather continues to cheer us ! And how sincerely do I feel your letters as cheering beyond even the smiles of the sun. He has been vehement, but is now only warm and comfortable, and rapid in his declension. I hope the lady-reformers will settle in *Libra,* and mind their shops again ; and weigh out the plums and suet for their puddings, ' as i' the olden time.' Let us keep disease from the *heart* of the nation ! One mob in the metropolis would frighten me more than *ten* at Manchester ; and *they* are held down safe for the present. But it is all very shocking, make as light of it as we will. What changes in our Bath society ! or, are they dreams? Some seem very black ones; not fit to be *shouted* perhaps, but *whispered* into the trumpet (of Fame to wit). Give me a hint, dear Sir, a taste merely of that stream of calumny which the Bishop of Meath said ' rolls down the streets of our favourite town, taking in a little fresh venom at every house it passes.' Adieu! and make my best regards acceptable to your lady and offspring : they are all very dear to their affectionate humble servant,

" H. L. P."

The Bishop of Meath, mentioned by Mrs. Piozzi, was O'Beirn, who has been some years dead. I heard the sermon in which he introduced the above-quoted passage on calumny. The figure of the stream is a happy one; but only of a piece with all his fine pulpit essays. His composition was invariably a rich specimen of the calm and correct in writing. His style, without being in the slightest degree gorgeous, was never less than elegant; his metaphors were never broken or misapplied; every word seemed to drop from his pen precisely in its proper place; and although each paragraph was in itself as finished as it could be,

he had scarcely an auditor in what is termed a refined
congregation, who might not have imagined that he
could have written exactly as the bishop wrote. To
this style his manner was admirably suited : in his
action and emphasis he was never theatrical, nor ever
tame; but, from first to last, abounded in gentle
earnestness : the whole discourse was in truth so
engaging, and so full of charms, that people used constantly to say what a pity it was that he made his
sermons so short; whereas he, in fact, never preached
for less than half an hour at a time. This feeling on
the part of his hearers was universal, and, no doubt,
a high compliment to his powers. The effect of what
he delivered, particularly during his latter years, was
heightened by his appearance. He wore not a little
greyish-blue wig, as English prelates do, but long,
flowing, snow-white locks; and had a face like Sterne's
monk, mild, pale, and penetrating; with a small,
sparkling eye, as brilliant and keen as a viper's; while
his voice, one of exquisite modulation, did all that
loudness and vehemence could have done, without
ever sounding as if raised to its utmost. He was
altogether a man of first-rate natural talents.

The vice of calumny, censured by the Bishop, may prevail in Bath, but not more so than in other idle towns. Besides, in Bath the essence of scandal, the *malus animus*, seems wanting. The good folks there are fond—not of detraction, but chattering; and would almost as soon speak well as badly of one another.

—

LETTER.—MRS. PIOZZI'S ACCOUNT OF HER-SELF, &c.

" Weston Super Mare, Sat. Night, Sept. 4, 1819.

" No indeed, dear Sir,—if I know myself, I am *not* low-spirited, nor disposed to think myself dying; though feelingly assured that if I lose health life must follow. At *my* age there is no time for sickness, and accommodations, and dispositions, and dawdling. My desire is to leave all straight and smooth behind me. But, as the boys say, there is a long account to *show up ;* and one must think of it whether one will or not. Johnson said we lived in a besieged town—all of us : and that we ought not to slumber at our posts, as if the enemy had retired from the ground. If so,

how much more vigilant should *we* be—*nous autres
octogenaires!   Our* slumbers must be like those of a
soldier sleeping on the attack. Life is a magic lantern
certainly ; and I think more so to women than to men,
who often are placed very early in a profession which
they follow up regularly, and slide on . with them life
labitur et labetur almost unconsciously.   But — we
females ! Myself, for example. I passed the first
twenty years in my father's and uncle's houses ;
connected with their friends, dwelling-places, and
acquaintances ; and fancying myself *at home* among
them.   No such thing : marriage introduced me to a
new set of figures ; *quite* new ; nor did I ever see but
distantly and accidentally any of the old group, or
their residences, from that day to this ; my mother
alone excepted.   She, indeed, lived near us for nine
years out of the seventeen I passed under Mr.
Thrale's protection ; and after wearing his name four
years longer, another marriage drove that set of
figures quite away, and I began the world anew,
with new faces around me, and in new scenes too :
for Wales was as much out of my usual beat, as Italy ;
my first husband having only seen enough of *it,* to

create aversion. I did, however, fancy, when Piozzi built a beautiful house on the estate and in the country my parents quitted in my early childhood, that I was got home again, somehow, though oddly. Quite a mistake was *that!* Bath *is* my home; and since I made it such, you, my dear Sir, who have so contributed *to sweeten it to my taste*, are really very kind in wishing me to set up my rest there. It is the safest and most proper place of abode for me.

" I thought London was to have run mad last week; but the fever of Reform is not yet hot enough. You will see that the great men who think they are making *Hunt* and *Co.* their tools to pull down one set of ministers, and put up another set which they can command, will themselves at length be used as tools by the multitude, who are honest in the avowal of *their* meaning, however absurd. *They* mean, like the wise men of Gotham, to pull the pins out of London-bridge, and *oil* them. And I remember wondering, when a baby, why that was thought so very foolish a project; for I doubted not but they wanted something, as we say, to be *done* to them! Indeed, a later adventure showed me how cautiously a work of reformation must be conducted: an old wall we wished to repair, down in Denbighshire, was all over-grown with ivy: ' cut it away,' said we; ' but,' replied an experienced workman, ' it has grasped the stones it loosened at the beginning; and if we cut it away, the whole will drop to pieces: the ivy now helps to support that wall to which it once clung for support itself.' So, I recollected the more serious allegory of the corn and tares, and let the business rest. The Octagon Chapel being shut up, as a *public place*, strikes me as comical! I shall be glad when you have either exposed or extinguished that fraudu-lent fellow, of whom it appears you have no small cause to complain. Those are among the vile vices one's heart most abhors, I think. *My* heart assures me your E. will never practise, or submit to such: he will be high-minded."

There is something curious in this letter on the subject of *Political Reform.* The paragraphs, in which, by the by, there is a great share of sound sense, devoted by her to the state of the nation, though so many years composed, appear as if recently written, and *since* the present agitating question had been discussed.

The shutting up of the Octagon Chapel in Bath for two or three weeks, is a circumstance occurring annually, and one which ought not to invite a sneer. Doctor Gardiner, the Minister of the Chapel, is a most regular and scrupulous performer of his duties; and is surely entitled to a few days of relaxation, as much as the clergy of the other places of public worship, many of which are annually closed, and not unfairly so, for a short time, as well as his Chapel.

The fraudulent person, who excited her indignation, was exposed as she wished; and as the Editor of the Bristol Mercury in 1819 will recollect. Mr. Manchee, the conductor of that paper, displayed much spirit, and showed great kindness to the aggrieved on the occasion. A man had attempted a literary imposture on the Editor of the " Bristol Mercury," a journal in great repute, and was speedily detected; being discovered to possess neither talents nor acquirements of any description. In speaking of this absurd transaction afterwards with Mrs. P., we naturally called to

recollection various instances of the kind. Such as
Lauder's assault on the fame of the immortal John
Milton, and Doctor Johnson's share in the business,
and subsequent excusable rage. Nor was Macpher-
son's simulation of antique Scottish poetry forgotten.
But both the criminals referred to were men of parts.
Ireland, too, had cleverness, as he proved, not by his
pretended imitation of Shakspeare, which does not
deserve to be called imitation, and is contemptible,
but by his vindication of himself, which is a very
entertaining book. From these delinquents we di-
verged to the ever-memorable affair of Chatterton.
When I asked her what was Johnson's creed on that
singular point of controversy, she repeated what she
had said elsewhere, in reply:—that Johnson to the
last declared the evidence to be so balanced, as to
leave the fact of the antiquity and authenticity of
Rowley's poems doubtful; but always said he could
not help thinking that Chatterton must have had a
coadjutor. Perhaps, had Doctor Johnson lived to
have read Doctor Sherwen's ingenious " Introductory
Essay," the herald of an intended publication on
Chatterton, &c., he would have been inclined to think

as the late admirable and venerable Doctor Haring-
ton, of Bath, told me he did; that though the so-named
poems of Rowley might not have been the work of
Rowley, they could not have been that of the modern,
unlettered boy, Thomas Chatterton.

———

LETTER.—TO MRS. ———.—TWO YOUNG GEN-
TLEMEN DROWNED, &c.

Weston Super Mare, Friday, Sept. 1819.

" My Dearest Madam,

" IN all parts of the world the same sad ' Winter's
Tale ' seems beginning; and the plague which Sir
James Fellowes stopped in Spain, has broken out again
at Cadiz. Meanwhile, I never saw such heavenly
weather; sunsets worthy of Cuyp and Claude; and
sea views fit for Vandervelde. The people, tedious;
the things, delightful. But Mr. —— must have the
remainder of my paper: my kind wishes and true
regards—all that is left of your poor H. L. P."

" My Dear Sir,

" I am ashamed of the low-spirited tone in which

L

I wrote my scrap to Mrs. ——. Here was an accident happened the other day, which surpassed all common cause of sorrow. Mr. Elton, son of Sir Abraham E., has lost two very fine young lads, swimming here among our rocks, three days ago. There was no danger in the place; a Newfoundland dog would have saved them; and I should scarcely have been alarmed for myself where they sunk, God knows how! No search has been successful in finding the bodies; and every one seems stunned by the event.

"With regard to the conspicuous miseries of the land we live in, let us thank God that the times we see are not like the times we read of. A Regent there, in history I mean, would take advantage of the mob's delusion, cajole the populace, rival Mr. H.; suffer him, however, and his adherents to destroy the Peers and Commons as an intermediate state; pronounce against their corruption, declare his resolution to reign in the hearts of his beloved people; take, with their assistance, money from the aristocracy of the realm, and rule, without a parliament, despotic!

" The bulk of mankind always like that form of government best; the mob can suffer one man's sway willingly; they hate that of five hundred, half of them uninformed as themselves, and risen from the ranks.

" A prince is commonly elegant in his manners; often amiable, and able to win over the minds of an assembled multitude, which naturally look up to pedigree as the most inoffensive cause of preference. It is not that he pretends to be wiser, handsomer, or stronger than we are : he and his fathers have been accustomed to rule; and so he shall sit in the seat of his ancestors.

" The deficit is a bad thing; but it might be proved, perhaps, that these complicated governments are more expensive than those where none claim to be paid for doing nothing. *Dragon à plusieurs queues* will slip through a hedge, where *Dragon à plusieurs têtes* would stick, and quarrel, and draw different ways.

" Poor, old Mr. L.! and I am sorry : they were kind to me, as you were, when kindness was valuable; and never shall my heart feel unaffectionate to their house. Doctor G. attends them, I know; but what can even dear Doctor G. do, when a man's hand is turned black with mortification, I suppose; or with

palsy, which immediately precedes it? They can
only try to keep him ignorant of his own danger, in
which attempt I see neither friendship nor good
sense; and beg earnestly that you, dear Mr. ——
will never practise such deception on

" Your H. L. P."

The dreadful domestic calamity mentioned in the
above letter, attracted more than ordinary notice at
the time, not only from the common operation of
human feelings, but the peculiar circumstances of the
sufferers.

The two young gentlemen so unhappily lost at
Weston, were youths of the fairest promise, and
justly the objects of pride and love to their parents
and kindred. They were the sons of a gentleman
admired as a scholar and a man of superior talents,
and most reputably known in the world of letters as
the elegant translator of Hesiod, &c. No sorrow
greater than that which overtook these bereaved
parents can well be imagined! According to the
affecting thought of the Greek philosopher, when the

young perish, the year may be said to have lost its spring! As Burke finely observes, the order of nature seems reversed; they who were looked to with confidence as posterity,' suddenly stand in the place of ancestry; and those who should have gone before, survive to bewail them. The parents destined to experience this agony, have not only to lament the dissolution of the beloved, but the downfall of long-cherished hopes; fond visions of all that was to be, and now can never happen. The victims of such a terrible visitation must never more expect one day, hardly one hour of unmixed enjoyment. It is woe of the deadliest kind, the poignancy of which time may mitigate, but cannot remove.

Mrs. Piozzi's opinion as to the cruelty of keeping the sick in ignorance of their danger, may be disputed. For my part, I should say that, generally speaking, it is the bounden duty of a discreet and tender friend to encourage the invalid to the final moment; and to leave him, if possible, at least the consolation of hope. In her own case, I certainly should not have complied with her injunctions, had I been so unfortunate as to have witnessed her dying hour; but I escaped the

misery which such a scene as that of her departure
would have caused, by the accident of leaving Bath,
just at the time of her being taken ill at Clifton, and
without being at all aware of her perilous situation.
That she was so herself, however, appears from what
has been stated in a foregoing part of these notes.

———

LETTER.—UNCERTAINTY OF LIFE; STEEVENS, THE COMMENTATOR, &c.

" Weston Super Mare, Monday, Oct. 4, 1819.

" YOUR letter, dear Sir, has lain too long unan-
swered. The horrible event of these young men's
death confined all conversation to one subject; and
that has been too soon changed for another very
striking occurrence. You know there is always in
such a place as this, a family which takes the lead;
one man that is looked up to. The magistrate, the
friend, the general benefactor at Weston, was Colonel
R., whose son, a gay young fellow, kept a pleasure-
boat, and used to make water-parties for us in the
warm weather. These gentlemen, distressed for the

loss of their young friends, were out in search of them; and on Thursday, 23d, I met them at a party, where the Colonel was cheerful, and boasted his prowess in staying so long, ten hours I think, upon the water. The man is dead now! Forty-three years old only; a fine, stout, manly person, and what some call very handsome. He caught a cold, and took a fever, and this morning died! Well,

> " Come he slow, or come he fast,
> It is but Death that comes at last.

Mr. L. lives, I understand; and that is strange to me; stranger perhaps, than that Colonel R. should die: less in the common course of nature. But, he wished to live, so I am glad.

" The Courier tells us C.'s life is in danger; so I suppose the young and strong are all to go, and leave us octogenarians. A Miss Case is first gone; an old acquaintance: we called her bonny Hester; Doctor Glass's sister in law: comely, cheerful, buxom; about forty: within very little of a handsome woman; agreeable to all. My daughter, Mrs H., has passed some time at this neighbourhood; we did not meet.

But, she met the clever Messrs. Smith, she says; and
one of them was very entertaining. She sent me a
stanza of a song he has written; but I dare say you
know it. If Mr. —— hears of it, he will claim
the authorship!

" The three black graces, Law, Physick, and Divinity,
  Walk hand in hand along the Strand, humming la poule ;
  Trade quits her counter, Alma Mater her Latinity,
  Proud again, with Mr. Paine, to go to school.
  Should you want advice in law, you'll nothing gain by asking it,
  Your lawyer's not at Westminster—he's busy pas de basquing it ;
  Would you wish a tooth to lose, and go to Wayte for drawing it,
  He cannot possibly attend—he's demi queue de châting it ;
    Run, neighbours, run ; all London is quadrilling it,
    Order and sobriety are dos à dos.'

Apropos to Mr. ——'s hardiesse, it is not new to
me ; and greater men have practised it. When Wilkes
and Liberty were at their highest tide, I was bringing
or losing children every year; and my studies were
confined to my nursery; so, it came into my head
one day to send an infant alphabet to the St. James's
Chronicle :—

    ' A was an Alderman, factious and proud ;
    B was a Bellas that blustered aloud, &c.'

"In a week's time Dr. Johnson asked me if I knew who wrote it? 'Why, who did write it, Sir?' said I. 'Steevens,' was the reply. Some time after that, years for aught I know, he mentioned to me Steevens's veracity! 'No, no;' answered H. L. P., 'any thing but that;' and told my story; showing him by incontestable proofs that it was mine. Johnson did not utter a word, and we never talked about it any more. I durst not introduce the subject; but it served to hinder S. from visiting at the house: I suppose Johnson kept him away.

"With affectionate regards to dear Mrs. ———, I remain ever your truly obliged and faithful

"H. L. P.

"We have left the hotel long ago; but it is all one with regard to the direction. The letters come in here at midnight, perversely enough."

———

October 11th, 1810, Mrs. P. returned to her house, No. 8, Gay Street, Bath.

The commencement of this last letter is " sicklied o'er " with the pale hue of melancholy. The dread of extinction, *i. e.* of leaving this state of being, and its associations, seems to have laid strong hold on the writer's mind. And, after all, nothing can be conceived more truly formidable than death to a person who, like her, possessed, in old age, brilliant intellectual faculties; who had seen so much of life in its most alluring form, and enjoyed with so keen a relish its highest pleasures!

Death was never with her a chosen subject, in our almost innumerable conversations; and I used sometimes to conjecture that she shunned it because she meditated on it so much and so awfully.

Shut our eyes to it as we may, it is obvious that the apprehension of death occupies the human feelings more than any thing else: it is that in which every one is interested, and almost all can equally well understand. She has indeed said to me, and the remark is nearly applicable to herself, that Johnson was afraid of dying, yet did not fear like a vulgar coward, but because his abundant learning, and the vast magnitude of his conceptions, assisted him to take a more expanded view than ordinary persons could do, of a question so important.

She, I am satisfied, reflected profoundly on death, also; but in this letter we see how she gets back to " this vile world" and its trifles; and takes refuge from sadness in the wit and pleasantry of one of the authors of the " Rejected Addresses." The lively stanza she quotes is in every body's recollection.

The story of Steevens and her " infant alphabet," is sufficiently singular; and seems to be combined with some misconception on the part of the fair authoress of the rhymes.   S. was a man of extraordinary abilities, and could have written the " Alphabet," or a better thing than it probably was: and although capable of mean acts, as Mrs. Hawkins avers, yet most likely the claiming of Mrs. Piozzi's lines for him, was rather Johnson's doing than his own.   I know nothing of the particulars adverted to by her, nor have I ever seen more of the " infant alphabet" than the couplet she transcribes.

LETTER.—ABSURDITIES OF PROTESTANT
CONGREGATIONS.

" *Saturday Night,*
" *Nov.* 27, 1819.

" I WISH, my dear Sir, I liked the state of my own
health, as well as I liked your ' Letter ;' (addressed
to the Bishop of Bath and Wells ;) it was much
wanted : a strange thing to confess in our enlightened
country.   But, I remember in Italy, when Mr. Chap-
pelow saw the good women on their knees, praying
most devoutly as some show passed by (which was by
no means connected with religion) ; he whispered one,
' What are these fools muttering about, as if their
salvation depended on it ?   We have no such ignorance in England ! '—' Nay, Sir,' was my reply,
' the same ignorance is exhibited all over England,
where we are exhorting, commanding, aye, and
absolving one another every Sunday of our lives : and
that species of ignorance you shall not find in Italy,
where the priest takes care to teach at least the sacred-
ness of his own functions, whatever he leaves untaught.'
But, dear Sir, you will find these follies increase

and not diminish, where every body teaches, as in Bath and London, and nobody learns. Where old women usurp the clerical profession, and catechise the poor children, without any form of sound words, to the destruction of St. Paul's command, ' let every thing be done decently and in order.' I hope the pamphlet will be a favourite."

The " Letter " which she took the trouble of reading, was a small pamphlet, published at Bath, in 1819, and addressed for form's sake, but most respectfully, to the then Bishop of Bath and Wells; by whom it was, of course, never seen; and if it had, would probably have been thrown aside, as beneath notice. Yet certainly the object it had in view was reasonable; that of exciting the attention of the diocesan, and others, to the manner in which portions of the church-service are usually delivered by the officiating clergyman; and the absurd manner in which congregations take part, during the performance of the sacred duties. What was strongly censured in the pamphlet, and the passage to which Mrs. P. particularly points, was an incredibly silly practice, witnessed at all times of public prayer, when the clergyman pronounces the "Exhortation." This address of the priest to the people, cannot be mistaken, by any one possessing the smallest share of common sense, for an appeal to the Deity. Yet is it carefully and piously repeated by his hearers; who with upturned eyes, and clasped hands, may be seen and heard going over the words " dearly beloved brethren, &c.," and "wherefore I pray and beseech you." Either they who thus recite words directed to themselves, as if words of thanksgiving or prayer, are fools ; or so shamefully regardless of what they are doing, and in whose sacred temple they stand, as not to affix any sense to the expressions they employ, or listen to. Repeating (as is constantly practised), the words of the decalogue, is equally childish and ridiculous, or, indeed, worse.

Not to think on such occasions is a mockery, to which it is the duty of the clergy to put a stop. They, it is to be hoped, are in earnest, and should instruct their flocks in the necessity of being in earnest likewise.

LETTER.—MRS. PIOZZI'S FETE.

" My dear Madam, your H. L. P. is thrown into perfect despair by the arrival of Lady Ramsay, to say how we have all been long engaged to meet.her at Sir Alexander Grant's dinner, on Thursday, 11th. I showed her your kind letter; but she says, and what is worse, says truly, that her uncle's card is of a prior date; and I said yes to it, on the very day Sir John and Lady Salusbury knocked at my door, and put everybody but themselves out of my head. Then came the fête, and put everything out of my head: and now, dearest lady, what will become of your distressed H. L. P.?"

" *Sunday, Feb.* 6, 1820."

———

The fête, which she says put everything out of her head, was a very memorable event in our annals of enjoyment at Bath.   It took place on January 27, 1820; and was a most sumptuous entertainment given by her at the Lower Assembly Rooms, to a company of between seven and eight hundred ladies and gentle-

men; whom, assisted by Sir John and Lady Salusbury, she received with a degree of ease, cheerfulness,
and polite hospitality, peculiarly her own. The occasion upon which this display of elegance and liberal
expenditure was made, was the completion of this
fascinating and extraordinary woman's eightieth year.
The festivity began with a ball, and concluded with
a costly and superbly arranged banquet. At the
latter, and at the top of the central table of three, our
amiable hostess presided, supported by a renowned
British Admiral of the highest rank on each side.
And, if anything could exceed the magnificent show
of the assemblage, glittering in the gayest attire, and
composed of all that Bath contained of exalted station,
talent, genius, youth and beauty, the profusion of
delicacies, lights, and jewelry; it was the gracious and
queen-like deportment of Mrs. Piozzi herself. Her
flow of disciplined animation seemed inexhaustible;
and her strength equally so: for, she had previously
opened the ball with Sir John Salusbury, and danced
with astonishing elasticity, and with all the true air
of dignity which might have been expected from one
of the best bred females in society.

I told her, and with perfect sincerity, that altogether such a victory of mind over matter, I had never witnessed; and she seemed pleased with the implied eulogy : but her mental qualities and bodily frame were, in every respect, out of the ordinary course.

In the month of July, 1820, she more than once walked from her house, 36, York Crescent, to the Mall, at Clifton, to visit us; a long and toilsome distance on a hot day, and such as any one would have thought oppressive. When I spoke of fatigue, and of my fears that she had done too much, she said, " No ; this sort of thing is greatly in the mind; and I am almost tempted to say the same of growing old at all ; especially as it regards three of the usual concomitants of age ; viz. laziness, defective sight, and ill-temper !" " Sluggishness of soul," she used to observe, " and acrimony of disposition, commonly begin before the encroachments of infirmity ; they creep upon us insidiously; and it is the business of a rational being to watch these beginnings, and counteract them." Her own power of sight was surprising: when past eighty, she has several times described minute features in the distant landscape we were viewing; or touches in a

M

painting, or engraving, which even sharp-sighted young persons failed to discover, and could only perceive when pointed out by her.

When I attempted to argue, and cried, " Dear Madam, surely we cannot prevent the decay of sight!" she would answer, " Perhaps not quite; but we may do much; every person, when about fifty, suffers an enfeeblement of the eyes; let not this be indulged, and let spectacles be resisted for a year or two, and the organ will, in great measure, retrieve its strength; and, depend upon it, accuracy of seeing means, very often, accuracy of looking, and, as Johnson has said, is much influenced by the understanding."

These were among her half-sportive, half-serious sallies; all of which I would gladly register, were it in my power, for admirable good sense invariably mingled with her pleasantry. Her more premeditated opinions, remarks, and inquiries made a deeper impression on my memory; and of these I shall introduce a few, in this the concluding portion of my memoranda, feeling reluctant to take leave of the subject of them, or to lose any thing associated with my recollection of one, to whom I am indebted for so many delicious hours of life.

ECLIPSE OF THE SUN.

Of this phenomenon, I copy the astronomical record as it lies before me:—

"September 7, 1820.—The sun eclipsed visible. Beginning 24 minutes past noon. Greatest obscuration, 1 hour 53 minutes. End 3 hours 17 minutes. Digits eclipsed 10 degrees 27 minutes. This eclipse annular in the Shetland Isles, and at Hanover, Frankfort, Munich, Venice, and Naples."

Relative to this eclipse, Mrs. Piozzi mentioned a singular fact. She said that when very young, and admiring a solar eclipse which occurred at the time, a medical gentleman and a man of science, the intimate friend of her family, was present, and observed that, from her general form, he thought she would be long lived, and might possibly survive to witness an eclipse of the sun, which would happen when she

M 2

would be about fourscore years of age; "and lo!"
she added, " here is the identical eclipse foretold, and
I have survived to see it!"

The effect of this phenomenon was extremely fine.
At twelve o'clock, the day was brilliant and warm;
and in about an hour and a half from that time, Bath
was wrapped in chilly twilight, or much such light, if
it can be so called, as remains between nine and ten
in midsummer. The small birds retired to housetops,
battlements, and the boughs of trees, and seemed to
sit dismayed; and the fearful and superstitious among
the poorer classes appeared awe-struck, and had re-
course to prayer. It was easy to conceive what
might have been the feelings of uncultivated men,
or of a whole people in a ruder age, on beholding
this solemn but natural occurrence in the planetary
system.

During the greatest obscuration, the sun looked
somewhat thus ◗

KEMBLE.

" *Thursday Night,* 13*th Jan.* 1817.

"I WILL not go to the play; I am not half well
myself; medicine will be better for me than Corio-

lanus to-morrow.   K. has acted King Lear to empty
benches."

———

I cannot, in strictness, say that I saw Kemble
play Lear at the Bath theatre, to what might be
termed a poor house; but I witnessed his Lear more
than once, when there was not such an attendance
as the effort deserved; for though not a part in which
he excelled, there were portions of it extremely striking
and beautiful; Kemble could not play any tragic character badly.   Still, in his hands, Lear was an unequal
personation; he seemed to aim at a contrast between
the beginning and the end; commencing as a tranquil,
venerable monarch, made shortly after justifiably angry
by the conduct of Cordelia; growing more and more
seriously violent, as his vexations increased; and at
last losing his wits from the overwhelming pressure of
his sorrows.

Young's Lear struck me as being more judiciously
conceived; and altogether always appeared to me a
finer portrait.   From the instant that he first tottered
out upon the stage, he intimated by his aspect, voice,
gait, and the quick clutching of his hands, that Lear

was one of those naturally irritable men, whom the
slightest contradiction would urge into wildness; and
who was already a peevish, half dotard, before the
capricious surrender of his dominions.   Young's art
then consisted in doing what I suspect Shakspeare
intended; in making Lear an object of the deepest
commiseration,—not as a dethroned, deserted king,
but as a wretched father, kindly, feeble, old, and
nearly friendless; and oppressed because he was such,
by the malignity of his persecutors.

MRS. PIOZZI'S AGE ; KEMBLE ; &c.

"*Jan.* 15, 1817.

"I AM not well; nor, I fear, going to be well directly;
but, ' be it as it may,' to-morrow is my seventy-sixth
anniversary, and I ought to be happy and thankful.

"The tick of the clock before Morton's execution is
certainly impressive; and Claverhouse's conversation
afterwards concerning death, and his own hoped-for
exit, comes in as a happy contrast.   My good wishes
will always follow Kemble; I have spent such pleasant

hours in his company. Poor fellow! But—once again 'be it as it may' I must think, and think seriously about

"Your obliged and faithful H. L. P."

In this letter of January 15, 1817, she marks her birth-day, and her advanced age, seventy-seven; and much about that time, I recollect her showing me a valuable china bowl, in the inside of which was pasted a slip of paper, and on it written, " With this bowl Hester Lynch Salusbury, was baptized, 1740." She was born on the 16th, or, as according to the change of style, we should now reckon, the 27th of January, 1741; and was certainly, as my readers must admit, a very extraordinary instance of a person of great mental endowments preserving her faculties unimpaired, beyond the period usually allotted for their continuance.

In speaking one day of the decay of the mind, she said she did not quite believe the fact; that is, she doubted whether or not dotage could steal upon one of a powerful intellect. I instanced Marlborough and Swift, and added what is repeated of the latter, who, when told that there was, somewhere, a very fine, intelligent old gentleman, worth going to see and converse with, replied, " No, there can be no such person ; had he possessed any great share of understanding, it would have been worn out long before this ! " She refused to listen to this plea, observing that Marlborough and Swift were probably, by a sudden occurrence of distemper, converted into idiots, which she admitted to be possible. But as to a mind of great original power, highly improved by cultivation, growing gradually imbecile, she almost thought it could not be.

MRS. PIOZZI ILL.

" Monday, April 14, 1817.

. . . . " I AM better than I was yesterday, though the *obituary* came into my head again at three o'clock this morning. I think your promise to take care of it would do good to yours, while

" H. L. P."

Here she employs the word obituary emphatically ; and in doing so, affords me, I trust, an excuse for the

present attempt to pay a tribute, however humble, to
her memory.

At the time of her lamented death, I was not only
absent from the place where it occurred, but was out
of England, and was thus prevented from attending to
what, I conceive, must have been her particular wish.
Her obituary article for the public journals was
written, as I have elsewhere stated, by her friend
Mrs. Pennington, of Clifton, a very ingenious and
well-informed woman, repeatedly mentioned in Anna
Seward's correspondence as the beautiful and agreeable Sophia Weston.

DR. JOHNSON'S IRENE.

" THESE are the lines I thought Dr. Johnson must
have had in his head, when finishing the second act of
Irene :—

········· " Prepare ye now for bolder deeds,
And know the prophet will reward your valour.
Think that we all to certain triumph move ;
Who falls in fight, will meet the blest above.
There in the gardens of eternal spring,
While birds of Paradise around you sing,

Each with his blooming beauty by his side
Shall drink rich wines that in full rivers glide ;
Breathe fragrant gales o'er fields of spice that blow,
And gather fruits immortal, as they grow :
Ecstatic bliss shall your whole powers employ,
And ev'ry sense be lost in ev'ry joy."

HUGHES'S SIEGE OF DAMASCUS.

Our Doctor has, however, improved upon them ; if
the last four lines can admit of improvement.

If you have not Irene (turn over), and read Mahomet's Address to the Lady :—

" If greatness please thee, mount th' imperial seat ;
If pleasure charm thee, view this soft retreat :
Here, ev'ry warbler of the sky shall sing,
Here, ev'ry fragrance breathe of ev'ry spring.
To deck these bow'rs each region shall combine,
And ev'n our prophet's gardens envy thine :
Empire and love shall share the blissful day,
And varied life steal unperceived away."

EDMUND BURKE, &c.

" BURKE, Pitt, and Fox, were three great men,
but utterly dissimilar. I knew neither of the latter
personally, but Burke intimately ; and if he deserved,

as no doubt he did, his public reputation only half as
much as he did his social pre-eminence, he must have
been a prodigy; for in private circles he had no equal."

In conformity to what she writes of Burke, she
invariably spoke of him as a man of singularly
agreeable manners: gentle, almost bashful, totally
devoid of affectation, especially of the affectation of
not being affected; either wanting in, or cautiously
shunning humour, but abounding in delicate wit, and
deep knowledge, literally, on every subject; and
possessing an inexhaustible stock of the most appropriate expressions, distant alike from Johnson's
pedantic language, or the lax prating in which Goldsmith indulged.

Unlike Mrs. Piozzi, I had witnessed their public
efforts, but had not any personal acquaintance with
two of the eminent men she refers to. They were
leaders whose transcendent talents will render them
objects of admiration to the human race, when not
only they who have known, and they who have seen
them, but their portraits and statues will have moul-
dered into dust.

In the spring of the year 1793, I remember seeing and hearing Edmund Burke speak a very long speech in Parliament; and can describe him as if he now stood before me. He was a tall and rather meagre man; and had somewhat stiff and uncouth in his air, probably through want of the habits of politeness; for in early life he had not kept the highest company. At the time I refer to, and when pointed out to strangers in the streets, as a renowned orator, states-man, and writer, he usually wore a blue coat, scarlet waistcoat, brown breeches, and grey worsted stock-ings; and a wig of fair curly hair, made to look natural. He also commonly used spectacles; so that it is not easy to describe his face. But I noticed that he had many wrinkles, and those more of thought than age. He had a double chin, as it is termed; large nostrils, a rather long, irregular nose, and a wide, and as it were, a loose mouth, such as many public speakers have. His speeches were always worth listening to; though his attitude was often unbecoming, as he would keep one hand in his waistcoat pocket, and the other frequently in his bosom, and swing his body from side to side, while his feet were fixed to one spot. Being an Irishman, he not only spoke with an Irish accent, which might be excused, but with an Irish pronunciation, for which there is no excuse; because English people of good education must needs know how to pronounce their own language; and when an Irishman of discernment and talents speaks differently, it must be because he chooses to do so, which is ridiculous. In spite of these objections, such were the charms of his eloquence, his words flowed in so grand a torrent, and he so abounded in happy metaphor and well-applied learning, that although I have heard him for several hours together, I do not remember being conscious of weariness or impatience, while he was on his legs.

Fox I first saw in the House of Commons in April, 1793; and knew who he was, as he advanced to take his seat on one side of the table, from the numberless caricatures of him which had long amused the idle world, in the shop windows. He was a man of middle height, fat and strongly formed. His skin was as yellow as that of Charles II,; he had also a very black, thickly-set beard, and large, bushy eyebrows,

which, pointing upwards, towards the centre of his
forehead, gave him the air of what he really was, a
man of great sharpness of understanding, much good
nature, irrepressible ardour, and many wild passions.
When speaking in parliament, or otherwise in public,
his action, and manner of standing, were sturdy and
ungraceful, and his voice was shrill and harsh.   He
was endowed with most splendid abilities, and his
labours as a statesman sat lightly on him, and had
little or no effect upon his temper, which was naturally
daring and gay.   That he could be merry on serious
occasions, is proved by various stories told of him;
and particularly by the circumstances attending his
duel with Mr. Adam, who shot Fox in the breast;
when, instead of appearing alarmed, he smiled and
said, he perceived it to be true that " Adam had
power over every beast of the field."   His friend in
the combat was Mr. Hare.   This actually did happen,
which is more than can be said of things related in
other old stories.   As to what Mrs. Piozzi says, in
writing of him, respecting his resembling Demos-
thenes, as far as dealing in close argument, in vehemence, and sarcasm, his eloquence was like that of

the renowned Athenian: but, when not highly excited, he was very heedless in the grammatical con-
struction of his sentences; and in these instances often
deeply indebted to the reporter.

When thoroughly warmed, he seemed inspired;
and then, nothing in oratory could exceed the correct-
ness of the passages he delivered, or equal his tremendous impetuosity.

Pitt was a tall thin man, of a fair skin, and with
rather an effeminate gait. He had light-coloured
hair, and grey, watery eyes, and a projecting sharp-
pointed nose, a little turned up. His forehead, in
the part nearest to his eyebrows, came far out, as
may be seen in his statues and busts; and to those
who are observers of human faces, gave the notion of
his being a man of the greatest possible clearness of
thought, and firmness of character; and such he proved
himself on every occasion. His manner of speaking
in the House (and I seldom heard him except in
parliament) was very lordly and commanding; he
generally stretched forth his right arm to its utmost
length, kept his left hand on his hip, or on the table,
near which he usually stood, and his feet at a proper

distance from each other, and spoke deliberately, like a person reading from a well-written book, and in a voice as loud and deep almost as a bell.

These sketches of the persons in question were shown to Mrs. Piozzi, with one of Richard Brinsley Sheridan subjoined; and she said they were rugged outlines, but gave her an idea of the men delineated.

Sheridan was above the middle height; his limbs were well formed, but rather heavy, and his shoulders somewhat round; he had one leg perceptibly larger than the other. His face, in the lower part, was fat, and all over too rosy for a very temperate or very discreet man. His eyes were most remarkable—large, of a dark colour, and shining, as if fire came from them; when near and immediately in front of him, few could bear to look steadily at his countenance. In pronouncing his orations, he had endless grace and variety of action; using both arms with such propriety, that by their movements one might nearly conjecture what he was saying. His voice had in it almost every sort of musical sound; it was sometimes as sweet as the notes of a violin, and at others as mellow as an organ. He was so great a master of original wit, rhetoric without rules, and natural eloquence of every kind, that he made those who heard him speak, believe him in the right for the time, be the subject of his oration what it might. He was, in short, neither moral, learned, nor wise; but so amazingly clever, that he completely imposed himself as such, upon his hearers, while declaiming either on the hustings or in parliament.

These rude outlines I had resolved to destroy; but an observation of Mrs. P.'s not only prevented that design, but has encouraged me to introduce them here. She said, " Keep them, by all means; they are coarse, but very strong likenesses of the mighty ones who are gone; keep them, because they may hereafter be made use of; besides, rely upon this as a fact, though it were hard to say why, that there is nothing about which the human mind of after-times is so eager as the bodily and mental lineaments of distinguished persons. The best parts of Aubrey's miscellaneous remains are his miniature pictures (daubs as they may be), of the great of his day."

LETTER.

" My Dear Sir,

" THE first letter I ever had from Doctor
Johnson is dated 1765. The regatta letter is in 1775,
after my mother's death, who disapproved of my
going into public so much, that I never did set my
foot in a theatre till my eldest child, born in 1764,
went with me to an oratorio.   No diamonds did I
ever possess."

―――――

This note is in reference to a story I had repeated
to herself, as told to me by an old lady of my acquaintance ; who, however, qualified the narrative by saying
that her memory was not good, and she might be
mistaken.   Her story was, that, when young, and
early in the reign of George III. she was one night
at Covent Garden Theatre, when a new married
belle was pointed out to her as Mrs. Thrale; and
that she could only recollect that the bride looked
lovely, and was adorned with diamonds.   The reply
on the part of Mrs. P. is characteristic, and undoubt-

edly contains the truth; so that her contemporary must have forgotten, or been misled.

LETTER.

" How could I be so stupid about the dolphins of Antium. I was at Torre d'Anzio myself, and saw the relics of a temple to Fortune, at the little place called Nettuno; the same lady whom Horace invokes, I suppose :

‘ O Diva! gratum quæ regis Antium.’

" Lord! how history and poetry do magnify matters! The first, a common mirror, perhaps; the second, a concave glass. Why, Torre d'Anzio is not above sixty or seventy miles from Rome; and she is mentioned by Ovid too, ‘ spissi littoris Antium;’ but I cannot find the place, though I know it is where a man is black-balled, and Hercules changes the colour of the lot he draws."

The passage referred to by Mrs. P. is in the 15th book of Ovid's Metamorphoses, line 718—

Et tellus Circæa, et spissi littoris Antium.

N 2

IMPROMPTU,

BY MADAME HOUDELOT, THE FRIEND OF J. J. ROUSSEAU.

La Nature, prudente et sage,
Force le tems à respecter
Les charmes de ce beau visage,
Qu'elle n'auroit pu repeter.

TRANSLATED BY MRS. PIOZZI, BATH, July 5, 1817.

ON THE DUCHESS DE LA VALLIERE.

Nature commanded Time to spare
The charms of lovely La Vallière ;
Knowing his course must be completed,
Before such charms could be repeated.

At different times she borrowed books of mine for
the purpose of reference : on one occasion a duode-
cimo volume, known as " Andrews's Anecdotes," and
" Dr. Sherwen's Introductory Essay on the Controversy respecting the Authenticity of Rowley's Poems."
Both of these, when returned, contained some short
notes by her on slips of paper, which I have carefully
preserved pasted in their proper places in the volumes
thus made valuable to me.   I also possess a gift of

her's, the three volumes 8vo. of D'Israeli's "Curiosities of Literature," in which are several marginal observations in her hand-writing.

A few of these specimens of her style of annotating may serve to amuse the reader.

———

ANDREWS'S ANECDOTES, &c.

" Many thanks for the pretty book, which you will at least see that I have read.

" Garrick wrote these words in his library at Hampton, in gold letters:—

' La première chose, quand on emprunte un livre,
C'est de le lire ; la seconde, c'est de le renvoyer.'

" I hope we shall have our box for Coriolanus ?
" 11th January, 1817."

———

Kemble was in the bills to play Coriolanus at the Bath Theatre, Thursday, 14th January, 1817, and announced as about to quit the stage.

" Dr. Johnson said Du Bellay's epigram

> ' Aboyant les larrons sans cesse,
> Muet pour l'amant favori ;
> J'étoit egalement cheri
> De mon maître et de ma maîtresse ; '

which he rendered thus, I remember,

> ' To robbers furious, and to lovers tame,
> I pleased my master, and I pleased my dame ; '

was originally a Greek one out of the Anthologia. It
is in every language : these are not printed quite
correctly ; I have read it in Spanish somewhere."

Du Bellay's epigram, as quoted by Andrews, is,

> " Latratu, fures excepi, mutus, amantes :
> Sic placui domino—sic placui dominæ."

———

" An idyllium of Theocritus, adapted to modern
times, by the ingenious Robert Lloyd."—ANDRS.

" Oh ! those old Sicilian gossips made into Mrs.
Scott and Mrs. Brown, by Bob Lloyd, are truly
charming ! I have seen them done very comically
into Italian."

" In the borough of Southwark is a sign on which is inscribed, 'The Old Pick my Toe.'"—ANDRS.

" So it is : I knew the sign, and was probably then the only person who could have guessed the derivation."

The figure in question represented the Roman slave looking for a thorn in his foot, after he had delivered a message of state importance. The original of the London figure is of bronze; it is finely preserved, and was to be seen in Paris, where the writer examined it in 1815.

THE MORAL COARSENESS OF OLD PLAYS.

" FARQUHAR'S making his Lord Aimwell offer Archer a choice between the money and the lady, is odd enough too."

OPERA OF ARTAXERXES.

" Great Augustus, long mayest thou," &c.

" THE reviewers justly remarked the absurdity of styling a king of Persia, Augustus."—ANDREWS.

" Augustus was an appellative, not a name; but the Persians had never heard it,—their mode of saluting royalty was Darius, i. e. Sovereign."

"LAWYERS mimicked by Mountfort, the actor, to amuse the Lord Chancellor Jeffries."—ANDREWS.

"I dare say the humour of making Portia, in the Merchant of Venice, mimic Lord Mansfield, came from this; 1 remember it always done."

———

"PERSONS of high rank, drinking to excess," &c.—ANDREWS.

> "The weather's cold, our Regent said,
>   Here fill me out a rummer;
> Till swallow after swallow made
>   The Prince believe 'twas summer."

———

"VERSES in four languages, written on the window of an inn, at Pont Bonvoisin;—

> "In questa casa troverete,
>   Tout ce que vous pouvez souhaiter;
> Bonum vinum, lectos, carnes;
>   Coaches, chaises, horses, harness."

———

"MR. OSBALDESTON, the great economist."—ANDREWS.

"This is all strictly true; Mr. Thrale knew the man personally, and invited him once to hunt with him at Croydon, that I might see so singular a character."

" LOPEZ D'ACUNHA, a gallant Spaniard," &c. —
ANDREWS.

" George the Third, not seeing well, touched the
sun-dial on Windsor Terrace somewhat roughly.
' Let it alone, your honour,' said the sentinel. ' Dost
not know me, soldier?' said the king. ' Yes, Sir, I
do,' replied the man, unmoved; ' but your Majesty
knows I must obey orders.' The addition to this is,
that the king gave the man a piece of gold."

———

" LE fameux La Galisse, chanson niais."—ANDREWS.

Andrews speaks of a sonnet borrowed from the
above; but as if ignorant of the author of " Madame
Blaize;" and Mrs. Piozzi's remark on the passage is,
" The lines are of Goldsmith's doing, but the humour
does not please in English."

———

SWIFT.

ANDREWS quotes the following lines by Swift, who
must, says Andrews, have been twenty-four years
old, when he wrote them: —

" The first of plants after the thunder, storm, and rain,
    And thence with joyful, nimble wing,
    Flew dutifully back again;

Who by that vainly talks of baffling death,
And hopes to lessen life by a transfusion of breath, &c.

"These," observes Mrs. P., "were the lines which led Dryden, when he saw them, to say, ' Cousin Swift, thou wilt never make a poet;'—a sentence, Johnson tells us, which the Dean never forgave."

I suspect some falsehood, or at least some strange mistake, in this story, repeated by Johnson and his friend Mrs. Piozzi. Such execrable lines could not have been written by him who was already the author of " a Tale of a Tub." And it is possible that there may have been some other writer of the same name as the Dean of St. Patrick's, to whom the composition referred to ought to be attributed. In that most extraordinary work, " Dunton's Life and Errors," 1 find, in the edition of 1705, Dunton acknowledging his obligations for articles sent to the " Athenian Oracle," to a " Mr. Swift, a country gentleman." But, in 1705, Dean Swift was thirty-eight years old, and known to the public, at least as an ecclesiastic.

PIRON.

" When a blind man begged of Piron the acade-
mician, as he came one day from hearing mass, at
Notre-Dame, he answered him in the words of Saint
Peter,

" ' Argentum et aurum non est mihi, quod autem
habeo, hoc tibi do.'

" So, taking out his tablets, he wrote these lines,
and pinned them on the breast of the blind man :—

> Chretiens! au nom Tout-puissant,
> Faites moi l'aumône en passant :
> L'aveugle qui vous la demande,
> Ignorera qui la fera ;
> Mais Dieu qui voit tout, la verra ;
> Je lui prierai qui vous la rende.'

> You that enjoy the light of day,
> Relieve a wretched blind man, pray :
> Unseen by me, your alms let fall,
> He sees them clear, who sees us all ;
> And when his rays remove all shade,
> In sight of all, you'll be repaid."

LETTER.—WITH A PRESENT OF D'ISRAELI'S
"CURIOSITIES OF LITERATURE."

" *Bath, April* 8, 1817.

" WILL you, my dear Sir, to the many kindnesses
you have shown me, add that of accepting these books,
which I at first bought for myself, and deformed with
notes on the margin. Afterwards, however, in a vain
humour, fancying you would like the manuscript nonsense along with the printed text, C. bound them, and
has made half the writing illegible to any one who
would not (as you do) know how to read, and always
with partial favour, the worst hand of your ever obliged
and faithful,

" H. L. PIOZZI."

" I would have inserted the Verses on a Watch-
Clock ; but that I think they are in Miss ————'s
scrap-book."

———

SIR ROBERT COTTON.—D'ISRAELI, VOL. I.

" MY first cousin, unlike to him, except in name,
Sir Robert Salusbury Cotton, father to this Lord

Cumbermere, burned all the Electress Sophia's elegant letters to his and my grandfather. I once saw them: she signed her name, I remember, with a long s, and there were many Latin quotations.

"H. L. P. 1817."

_____

LOUIS XIV. AND CORNEILLE.

" The king knew he had killed him with unkindness : the poet had presumed on his Majesty's attentions, aud wished to give political advice, which Louis would not endure."

_____

DOCTOR DEE.—Temp. Eliz. and Jas. I.

" Doctor Dee was a quack and an astrologer; and pretended to tell fortunes. His name was not Dee, but he called himself so, as professor of the black arts: Dee in the Cambro-British tongue meaning black: the river Dee is the black river. The Doctor was a Welshman. A piece of

black basalt belonging to him, is now at Strawberry
Hill—1817."

SAMUEL BOYCE.

" DOCTOR Johnson used to beg for him ; but did not
relate, till after his decease, how, when he had pro-
cured a guinea, and laid it out in roast beef and port
wine, Boyce quarrelled with him, because he had
forgotten their favourite sauce; "and how can a
man eat roast-beef," said he, "without mushrooms,
or catsup."

LYDIAT.

" THIS," says D'Israeli, " was that learned scholar
whom Johnson alludes to ; which allusion was not understood by Boswell and others."

" Very true; Lydiat's life, and Galileo's end, is
the line referred to."

ERASMUS IN A POST-CHAISE.

" ON horse-back : there were then no post chaises."

HAGLEY.

" THE Lord of Hagley used to send his visitants to see the Leasowes, directing them in at the wrong door, that so they might read the inscriptions backwards ! ' These little things are great to little men,' says Goldsmith."

THE PINELLI LIBRARY.

" D'ISRAELI states that the ' books of this splendid library, being shipped for Naples, and seized on the passage by pirates, were all thrown into the sea.'

" Edwards of Pall Mall, however, and Robson of Bond Street, bought a few; and I believe Lord Spencer has them."

APOLLO AND MINERVA
ON THE TOMB OF SANNAZARIUS, IN A CATHOLIC CHAPEL.

" THIS is the joke, one hundred times repeated, on Sannazarius's tomb ! But why do we not laugh at Hercules and Minerva on General Wade's, or General

Fleming's tombs, in Westminster Abbey? I think
there it is worse."

THE RIVER PO.

"THIS river is so rapid, that Tasso says of it:

Pare
Che porti guerra e non tributo al mare.

" And Miss Seward says that our little river Dee,

As o'er the rocks it raves,
Brings terror and not tribute to the waves."

FINIS.

" A PROLOGUE was presented by one French wit to
another, for correction and advice. ' Sir,' replied his
friend, 'there is but one letter wrong; instead of
saying, fin du prologue, let us print it, fi du prologue.' "

VORAGINUS.

"VORAGINUS was so called from Voragine, a gulf,
which swallows all; as Erskine's book styles London,
Swaloal."

ANAGRAM.

"There is a comical story in the world, of Sir Roger L'Estrange going to see Lee, the poet, when confined for lunacy. The first expressing his concern to see his old friend in so dull a place, 'Ay, Sir,' replied the other,

'Manners may alter, circumstances change,
But I am Strange Lee still, and you Le Strange.'"

"The prayers of the great are so many orders."—D'Israeli.

"It should be requests; when kings are forced to pray for civility, they are sure to be refused."

TITLE.

"D'Israeli says, 'I find two verses in my copy of Selden's Titles of Honour, in an old handwriting, which I think worth preserving:—

'And never yet was title did not move,
And never eke a mind that title did not love.'

o

A thought borrowed by Shenstone, in his Schoolmistress, the expression scarcely changed."

The lines in the Schoolmistress, referred to by
Mrs. Piozzi, are—

" For never title yet so mean could prove,
But there was eke a mind which did that title love."

QUEEN SHEBA.

" The Queen was called Shebeh, because she was
Queen regnant, not consort. Shebeh is a sceptre;
she swayed it in her own right."

FASHION.

" Aimwell and Archer, in Farquhar's Play, talk
much on the subject of wigs; and I remember Garrick
dressing the wig on the stage, and saying, ' This is
the most obstinate curl!'"

NATURAL PRODUCTIONS.

" There was a Count Rombassome, who, about fifteen years ago, showed a Labrador stone, with the effigies of Louis Seize upon it;—his crown dropping off and ' gouts of blood ' visible round the neck.   He sold facsimiles of it for one guinea each; I bought one, and set it in a seal for Lady Williams.   The original was much admired, till somebody said it was helped out, and then the whole story faded away."

———

FARINELLI AND THE POWER OF MUSIC.

" This is making a wonder of no uncommon occurrence.   The King of Spain was melancholy, in consequence of his wife's death; and to hear the song she was fond of, sung by Farinelli, soothed his sorrow. After the King was in bed every night, Farinelli was regularly called to execute that particular air, ' Per quel caro amplasso!'   And it goes by the name of ' Il Re di Spagna ' now, among Italian professors of music."

CURIOSITIES OF LITERATURE.—Vol. II.

LITERARY FOLLIES.

" Example :—

Sometimes I've a head, and sometimes I've a tail,
And sometimes I am seen without either ;
The Judge I adorn often sends me to jail,
Yet the thing I most hate is bad weather.
When contracted to ladies, I sit close and sly,
Renouncing my very existence ;
When expanded by wisdom, I meet your broad eye,
And some wise men have own'd my assistance.
Yet, on night's near approach, here your pardon I beg,
I exchange Doctor Parr for my dear little Peg."

LITERARY CONTROVERSY.

" A lady, not at all a lady of affectation, repri-
manding her coachman for getting drunk, read to him
the story of Alexander killing Clytus, with proper
comments; and in so impressive a manner, that the
fellow burst into tears, and promised he would never
get drunk again. I wondered, when she told me, that
the man did not laugh at her, instead of crying for old
Clytus."

"A Welsh bishop made an apology to James I. for preferring the Deity to his Majesty."—D'ISRAELI.

"Qu. who was he?"

I am unable to answer Mrs. Piozzi's question; but D'Israeli's story might have been told of Dr. Neale, Bishop of Durham: for, when James I. asked the Bishop of Winchester and him, " My Lords, cannot I take my subjects' money when I want it, without all this formality of Parliament?" the Bishop of Durham readily answered, " God forbid, Sir, but you should; you are the breath of our nostrils."

See Johnson's Life of Waller.

LOVE AND FOLLY.

" WHEN Love and Folly went to play,
Upon a sun-shine holyday,
    Poor Cupid cried, be quiet;
Have done, you silly creature,—do;
Romping's unsafe with such as you:
    I'm blinded in this riot.
Straight to Olympus they repair:
' Nay, if he fell in Folly's snare,'
    Bright Venus quickly cries out;

'Let her henceforward be his guide ;'
'Right, right ;' old Jupiter replied,
'"Twas she that put his eyes out.'"

This annotation by Mrs. P. relates to a "Morality" by Louise L'Abbé, the Aspasia of Lyon, in 1550: the title is "Debat de Folie et d'Amour."

ABRIDGERS.

"A LADY once asked me at Streatham Park, to lend her a book. 'What sort of a book would you like ?' said I. 'An abridgment,' was the unexpected reply; 'the last pretty book I had was an abridgment.'"

OBSCURITY.

"BURKE said it was a source of the sublime."

DR. HAWKSWORTH'S VOYAGES.

"HE got so large a sum of money for the work, they never suffered him to enjoy it for an hour !" And

Mrs. P. adds, " his lamentable death was the result
of the persecution he underwent."

FURETIERE.

" FURETIERE wrote the pretty French chanson à boire
from which was imitated our ' Tippling Philosophers.' "

THE DREAM OF PATRIS, THE POET OF CAEN.

" THIS is imperfectly quoted by D'Israeli ; Here
are the verses :—

> Je songeois cette nuit, que de mal consumé,
> Cote-à-cote d'un Pauvre on m' avoit inhumé ;
> Mais que ne pouvant pas souffrir le voisinage,
> En mort de Qualite je lui tins ce langage :
> Retire toi, Coquin,—va pourrir loin d'ici,
> Il ne t'appartient pas de m'approcher ainsi ;—
> Coquin ! me repondoit-il d'une arrogance extrême :
> Va chercher tes coquins ailleurs, Coquin toi-même ;
> Ici tous sont egaux ; je ne te dois plus rien :
> Je suis sur mon fumier—comme toi sur le tien.

> I dream'd that in my house of clay,
> A beggar buried by me lay ;
> Rascal ! go rot apart, I cried,
> Nor thus disgrace my noble side !
> Rascal yourself ! the corpse replied ;

I owe you nothing : look not sour ;
Death levels all, both rich and poor ;
Lie still then, Friend, and make no more ado ;
I'm on my dunghill here—as well as you."

SCARRON.

" Who addressed one of his dedications to his Dog."

" Hannah More wrote an Ode, in former days, to Garrick's dog, Dragon."

ROMANCES.

" We have a singular story in Wales, of a man who married a fairy, and called her Penelope.   She told him that the touch of cold iron would be fatal to their happiness.   But he fell from his horse one day, when they were riding out together, and the horse ran away. Our lovers forgot their caution : he threw the bit and bridle, so that the bit touched her finger; when, like Eurydice, she disappeared, and was lost to him for ever."

JAMES I.

D'ISRAELI relates the treacherous conduct of this most contemptible fellow, King James I. towards the Earl of Somerset; calling out to the Earl, on whose disgrace he had determined at the time, " For God's sake, when shall I see thee again!" &c. On which passage Mrs. Piozzi's remark is a quotation of the very words used by James in the hearing of his servants, before the Earl had well turned his back. " Ah blessed be God, I shall never see thee more. " " Hypocritical monster!"

James I. said " Were I not a King, I would be a University-man."—D'ISRAELI.

" And the honourable Thomas Fitzmaurice, father to the present Lord Kirkwall, said he would—if not a linendraper—be provost of Eton!"

GENERAL MONK'S WIFE.

" SHE had been his cook; and when he was refractory, she was wont (says some old book) to beat his good Grace with the ladle."

MODES OF SALUTATION, &c.

" OF which, and of their origin, the wisest account
is in the ' Fable of the Bees.' "

FIRE-WORKS, AND TORRE, THE ARTIST.

" WHEN Torre was in England, he exhibited some
beautiful Pantomimes in fire, at Marybone Gardens.
Venus begging armour of Vulcan for Æneas, I remember ; and Theseus, (Hercules, I mean,) dragging
Pirithous from hell. The artist was imprisoned soon
after for gross immorality. ' He may now (said Steevens to my father) organise a new fire-work !' "

INFLUENCE OF NAMES.

HERTZ SCHWARTS.

" IT was Schwartsfield, black-field, or, as we say,
black-lands. Casaubon was a name of the same kind:
his family appellation was Beaujardin, and he sometimes does call himself Hortibonus. Doctor Johnson
said Albinus's anatomical tables were the work of a
Mr. White, who latinised his name at the University

of Leyden.   A Mr. Black, his friend, called himself Nigrinus, and the people laughed at him."

CURIOSITIES OF LITERATURE.—Vol. III.

THE PANTOMIMICAL CHARACTER.

" D'Israeli expresses his wonder as to how the Latin word Sannio was converted into the Italian Zanni, &c."

" The Latin Sannio makes the Tuscan Giovanni, which Venetians speak and write Zanni: thence a zany, a fool, a *jean-potage*, a jack-pudding."

MR. PUNCH,

" In Italy, denominated Policinello, a little flea: active and biting, and skipping; and his mask, puce colour; the nose imitating in shape the flea's proboscis."

HARLEQUIN.

" When Arlecchino, a native of Bergamo, crossed

the Alps to France, he became Harlequin; and they
said, or fancied, that there was an allusion to *Charles
Quint*."

LAZZI, A SPECIES OF BUFFOONERY.

" Whence Lazzagnetti, a sort of flat maccaroni
which these drolls pretended to spit out of their
mouths; for in all these exhibitions no delicacy was
ever admitted to destroy mirth, or rather gross merriment."

THE ITALIAN THEATRE.

See in D'Israeli a curious account of what is
called a " platt," *i. e.* a paper of stage directions for
the arrangement of a sort of pantomime in Elizabeth's
times; in which is found " Pantaloon, and his man
Peascod, with spectacles." Steevens supposes this
explains the passage in " As You Like it; " " the lean
and slippered pantaloon, with spectacles on nose."
Mrs. Piozzi observes, " Certainly slippered; he runs
after Harlequin, and cannot catch him, as he runs in
slippers."

MASSINGER, &c.

" Massinger, and Molière, and Ben Jonson, all make the business of their play, whatever it is, subservient to one leading character . the other people are as nothing but figurantes. Mr. Luke, Sir Giles Overreach, Volpone, and the Malade Imaginaire, attract and detain your attention from all the other characters."

———

" ' White figs in England as good,' says Sir William Temple, ' as any of that sort in Italy.' The art of cultivating them must have been lost; for our figs now resemble not in any wise those of Italy."

———

CHIDIOCK TITCHBOURNE, AND TOM SALUSBURY.

" Tom was an ancestor of mine. The Queen's (Elizabeth's) grant of pardon to Salusbury, not Salisbury, as D'Israeli prints it, is in my nephew's possession now; her majesty's figure delineated on the parchment. H. L. P. 1817.

" The name was originally Saltsbury, from Adam

de Saltsburgh, son of Abraham, Duke and Prince of
Bavaria. In the year 1070, his adventurous spirit led
him to England with William the Conqueror, who
gave him in Lancashire ' a fayre house,' says the
pedigree, ' called Saltsbury Court.' "

" The Queen (Elizabeth,) was greatly ' angried.'—
' Angered: '—the other never was an English word."

COURT CEREMONIES.

" In the court of James the First, a stool at the
end of the table was reserved empty, for state."—
D'Israeli.

" Thence came the ' honours of the *Tabouret.*' "

NAMES OF STREETS IN LONDON.

PICCADILLY BEING ERRONEOUSLY EXPLAINED BY D'ISRAELI.

" Piccadilly was named from a Dutch word, Pick-
adil, the hem, or outskirt of the town ; as it was, in
King William the Third's time. Lord Burlington
used to rejoice that he lived where nobody could go
beyond him."

PURIM PLACE.

" Not long ago, a Hebrew, who had a quarrel with his community, built a neighbourhood at Bethnal-Green, and retained the subject of his anger in the name the houses bear, of Purim Place. This may startle some theological antiquary at a remote period, &c.— D'Israeli.

" He will *start*, because Purim means Lot in Hebrew; so the man, having quarrelled, he knew why, with his neighbours, called it, half in anger, half with delicacy, Purim Place; he would not say Lot's Place."

DRINKING IN ENGLAND.

"Et quocunque deus circum caput egit honestum. Georg. ii. 392.

" Honnete, in French, renders the Latin exactly."

TOM O' BEDLAM.

" When I was about twelve years old, I remember James Harris, of Salisbury, and my dear old friend and tutor, Doctor Collier of the Commons, talking, and telling of a man they called Dowdie, who diverted the townsfolk of Salisbury by personating a lunatic, to amazing exactness; and when a young blustering fellow came to the inn, it was their sport to frighten him with Dowdie. This went on, I think, till some foreign gentleman ran the mock bedlamite through one arm with his sword; and after that he would play Dowdie no more."

CHARLES I. AND HIS DIAMOND SEAL,

MENTIONED BY HERBERT.

" A DIAMOND is a diamond only because of its hardness. I question whether any tool can engrave on a good diamond. I once saw an emerald of oriental birth, and great value. Its owner told me it was almost a diamond, and he would have it engraved. The work cost him fifty-eight guineas, and the gem was much reduced in size. It was so hard it ruined every tool that touched it, and the figure on it was ill expressed after all."

THE GOODS, &c. OF CHARLES I. SOLD BY ORDER OF THE COUNCIL OF STATE.

"I saw a cabinet at the Colonna Palace, in Italy, which had belonged to Charles I., and they seemed in 1786, to esteem it very highly."

THE DUKE OF BUCKINGHAM.

"There is a very pretty, quaintly-expressed letter of Howell's to the Favourite, saying he would stand more surely without an anchor, &c.; meaning that he should give up his place of Lord High Admiral."

JOHNSON'S LIFE OF POPE.

Doctor Johnson says of Pope, "he has a few double rhymes; but always, I think, unsuccessfully, except once in the Rape of the Lock."

The concluding comment by Mrs. Piozzi on D'Israeli's work, is

> "The meeting points the fatal lock dissever,
> From the fair head—for ever and for ever;

was the couplet Johnson meant, for I asked him, and he said so. "H. L. P."

P

DOCTOR SHERWEN ON CHATTERTON.

Doctor S. says in his preface to "an Introduction,
&c." that "the grossness of an error is not the less for
the number or respectability of its supporters."

Mrs. Piozzi observes in the margin of my copy of
the "Introduction," "Well, if a thousand, or if ten
thousand people joining in a blunder, hinder it not from
being a blunder, what will become of a common newspaper and even parliamentary phrase, 'under these
circumstances'? For, though a man may be under
correction, or under the rod of affliction, he cannot
well be *under* circumstances, which, to be such,
must necessarily *stand* around us."

SWARTE,

WHICH IN GERMAN MEANS BLACK.

"Swart in the German tongue is black, certainly.
The real name of Melancthon was Swartsfeld; as we
say Blacklands. They Grecised the word at his
university."

FUSELI'S NIGHT MARE.

" It is long since I saw Fuseli's night-mare, which appeared to me a sort of undefinable thing with a head of stone: or not unlike the bony skeleton of a mare's, or horse's head; it impressed me, I remember, with precisely the feelings he wished. ' Les meres de nuit,' is a most elegant explanation, and to me — new."

The explanation is Doctor Sherwen's, and undoubtedly an instance of very happy conjectural criticism. Nothing can be conceived more absurd than Fuseli's mistake, and that of multitudes more learned than the painter, on this subject.

ROUGE.

I shall here endeavour to comment, as far as I can, on several points in my Piozziana, upon which I may not have sufficiently enlarged in their proper places; if any place can be supposed less proper than another, in such an olio as this.

When Mrs. Piozzi sat for the miniature picture

which she gave me, she directed the artist to represent her as wearing rouge: and this unnatural colour is very discernible in the painting. She carefully put it upon her cheeks every day before she went out; and sometimes before she would admit a visitor—or sometimes in his presence. One day I called early at her house; and as I entered her drawing-room, she passed me, saying "Dear sir, I will be with you in a few minutes; but, while I think of it, I must go to my dressing-closet and paint my face, which I forgot to do this morning." Accordingly she soon returned, wearing the requisite quantity of bloom; which, it must be noticed, was not in the least like that of youth and beauty. I then said that I was surprised she should so far sacrifice to fashion, as to take that trouble. Her answer was that, as I might conclude, her practice of painting did not proceed from any silly compliance with Bath fashion, or any fashion; still less, if possible, from the desire of appearing younger than she was, but from this circumstance, that in early life she had worn rouge, as other young persons did in her day, as a part of dress; and after continuing the habit for some years, discovered that

it had introduced a dead yellow colour into her com-
plexion, quite unlike that of her natural skin, and
that she wished to conceal the deformity. In this
there was something rational; but, what can be
imagined more ridiculous than the attempt of common
minds, in the female world, to hide the effects of the
encroachment of time? The beauty of old age—and it
has beauties peculiar to itself—consists in being, in all
respects, as unlike youth as possible. At seventy,
paleness and silver hair are ornamental; but there is
somewhat unutterably shocking, and worse than taste-
less, in the countenances of many of the old ladies to
be met with in such profusion, at card-parties and
elsewhere: something hideous in the conflict carried on
in their visages, between wrinkles and roses: eyes
half extinct, and glossy ringlets of purchased hair.
And may it not be asked, why should that system of
juvenile dressing be thought proper in general life,
which would be considered inadmissible on the stage?
There, when sympathy is to be called forth, the
costume of the old, however at variance with times
and manners, is calculated to imply the seriousness,
dignity, worth and weakness, of declining years: and

Mrs. Heidelberg, Lord Ogleby, Mrs. Hardcastle, &c., are arrayed in youthful finery, that they may be laughed at.

SANTERRE.

MRS. PIOZZI mentions the name of this remarkable man, and adds an anecdote of his having a horse belonging to him, stabbed by an insolent courtier, before the revolution, &c. What was the primary cause of his becoming a violent republican, it would now be difficult, if not impossible, to discover. But she assured me that in private circles he appeared to be a person of strong natural sense, and great plainness and sincerity of character. If so, he could not have deserved the reproach with which his memory has been stigmatised in the history of the times.

He commanded, as every one knows, the guards which surrounded the scaffold, when Louis XVI. was put to death; and has since been consigned to infamy, for the cruel act of ordering the drums to beat loudly, and thereby preventing the people from

hearing the words of the wretched king, when about
to address them. He has, however, been thoroughly
and ably exculpated, in an account, published by an
English traveller, of a visit to France made by him
early in the century; I am not sure, but I think the
name of the writer is King: his defence of General
Santerre is as follows. He was introduced to him,
and found him returned to his original occupation of
brewing. They conversed till the stranger discerned
that Santerre was such a man as Mrs. Piozzi described
him; and so candid, and apparently incapable of inhu-
manity, that he designedly started the subjects of the
revolution, and the execution of Louis; bluntly telling
the other what was generally reported and believed.
His answer was, that the report was perfectly correct;
that he had ordered the drums to beat, expressly to
hinder Louis from being heard; for which his reason
was, that, on the eve of the day of execution, he had
ascertained the existence of a conspiracy of many hundred young men, who had agreed to meet in the Place
de la Revolution, armed, and provided with signals by
which to recognise each other; and that as soon as

the King should have spoken, they were simulta-
neously to make an attempt to rescue him. "This,"
proceeded Santerre, "I knew must end in a dreadful
tumult, the loss of multitudes of people, the defeat of
the Royalists, and the death of the monarch; for I
had present, and in a state of thorough discipline,
sixty thousand troops, who would, I was sure, do their
duty, and obey the Assembly : to prevent this scene
of horror, I acted as I did; and applaud myself for
having done so."

This is probably a true statement; the action performed, and the motives, are consonant to the ordinary
principles of human conduct; while the brutality
alleged against Santerre is contrary to these principles,
and improbable : no bad rule, perhaps, whereby to
judge of the force of testimony in general.

MACKENZIE, AND SIR WALTER SCOTT.

MACKENZIE certainly had merit as a writer of pe-
riodical essays ; but his fame seems to have been

founded chiefly on his "Man of Feeling," which, after
all, if carefully examined, would not endure the scrutiny of criticism. It is, however, a prime favourite
with young novel-readers; and, as far as morals are
concerned, "there is no offence in it." There is less
foolishness, and more regularity of story in his " Man
of the World; " though Boswell reports that Doctor
Johnson, having read the work, said he saw but little
in it; and Mrs. Piozzi used the same expression, in
speaking of the book to me. Still, she gave high
praise to Mackenzie, and much higher to Sir Walter
Scott, to whose name, the mention of Scotland, and
Scottish writers, naturally led us. When this conversation occurred, early in 1815, the author of
" Waverley" was unknown, but eagerly guessed at;
and I could, at the time, in some measure, have assisted
conjecturers in their search, owing to the following
circumstance, which, strangely enough, then escaped
my recollection.

In the summer of 1804, being at Edinburgh, and
walking one evening with a friend in the suburbs, we
were joined by Sir Walter Scott, to whom I had
been previously known, and to whom indeed I was

indebted, during my residence in the Scottish capital,
for numberless polite and hospitable attentions; and
for many a cheerful hour most pleasurably passed in
his society. In the course of our walk, we reached a
handsome house, the door of which was open, and an
elderly, thin man, without his hat, was standing on
the steps in front. Either my friend, or Sir Walter,
I now forget which, but to the best of my belief it
was Scott, turned to me, and said, "you must be presented to our Scottish Addison—Mr. Mackenzie,"
who immediately honoured me with his hand. Long
after this, came out " Waverley;" with a Dedication,
not, as usual, prefixed, but at the end of the concluding page, " To the Scottish Addison, Henry
Mackenzie." When I saw this, it forcibly brought
the past to my mind; the epithet, so applied, created
a suspicion as to the unknown author; and this,
though not direct, is an instance of very strong cir-
cumstantial evidence, such as in a court of justice
would have almost produced conviction ! Notwithstanding this, I was myself, for several years,
doubtful, or rather I had adjusted the difficulty, by
supposing that some one, intimate with Sir W. Scott,

must have been the writer of the far-famed Novels and Romances; and that these had been occasionally submitted for correction, augmentation, &c., to Scott.

My reasons for entertaining doubts of his claims to the labours of the undisclosed author, were, according to my conception, not only cogent but unanswerable; namely, the profusion of bad writing which appeared in the so much talked-of works, mingled with some of the most splendid passages, both as to fancy and style, which the English language can show. But I close this article here : to specify the errors alluded to, would be an unwelcome office to me, and to others; to enlarge, with sufficient praise, on the beauties in the pages of him who wrote " Waverley," impossible.

Sir Walter Scott has recently been taken, by the stroke of fate, from the country his genius adorned; and the sale of his books has increased since the occurrence of this really national calamity. His fame will probably last longer than that of most eminent men; certainly longer than that of any so admired during life as he was. Such full renown as he enjoyed, is generally reserved for the memory of the mighty.

How trivial was the reputation of the living Shakspeare, compared with what now attends the mention
of his imperishable name !

———

COSTUME.

At every opportunity which presented itself, Mrs.
Piozzi was the strenuous advocate of the present day,
in opposition to the past; and in defiance of a prevailing and very long established weakness among old
people, that of supposing every thing now worse than
what it was formerly. On the contrary, she always
maintained, that " nothing but ignorance or forget-
fulness of what our grandfathers and grandmothers
generally did and suffered, not politically, but in
matters of dress, behaviour, &c., could incline any one
to entertain a doubt as to the fact of modern improvement in most of the essentials of life." This, she
would say, was especially true with regard to our
habiliments; and used to expatiate very agreeably,
not only on the absurdities of the habits usually worn
in her early days, but on the consequent embarrass-

ments in which the artists of the age were involved;
pointing to miniature pictures of the times, then before
us, or to engravings of celebrated paintings, executed
to commemorate some occurrences of great public
interest. She thus often made infinite sport for herself and me, by her comments. For instance, she
called the famous " Death of Lord Chatham," (who,
as my reader must recollect, is represented fainting in
his place in the House of Peers,) " a record of wig-
gery ; " and laughed excessively at the rueful effects
produced on the different physiognomies of the sur-
rounding crowd of distinguished men in this composition, by the mass of wigs presented to the spec-
tator's eye, the incredible variety of human ugliness
they exhibit, and the utter impossibility, on the part
of the painter, to do justice to the requisite expression
of countenance in heads surmounted by such execrable
articles of costume as full-bottomed perukes.

THEATRE.

FROM many passages in her letters, it appears that
the playhouse had always great attractions for Mrs.

Piozzi, and this her conversation confirmed. She was, in fact, on the reasonable side of enthusiasm, among the fondest votaries of the amusements of the stage; and defended her partiality, by what seemed to me arguments equally ingenious and solid　I have myself constantly been so great an admirer of the drama, that I own I was highly pleased to have my taste sanctioned by a person such as she was. The truth is, that the stage has been basely calumniated. To apply, in substance, what I have said elsewhere more diffusely, it would be easy to prove that a prejudice against the stage is, to the utmost degree, illiberal and unjust; and that the greatest injury which, for many years, the public mind has suffered, has been inflicted by the opponents of the drama. The unthinking, and wrong-headed among these, know nothing of the moral power of the stage, and its supporters; and have, unwittingly, lent their aid to its enemies of another description, the self-styled Righteous; who are, in reality, and with a view to their own advantage, the foes of every system by which the human intellect can be enlightened, or the human heart improved; the foes of that stage, for which

the prince of poets, and moralists,—Shakspeare,—
composed his immortal scenes; which has been graced
by the Muse of Steele, and Addison, and Thomson;
for the adornment of which, and to advance its noble
ends, the wisdom, and wit, and genius of this une-
qualled country, England, have been for centuries
exerted. That stage, which, be it remembered, found
its steadiest and kindest patron in George the Third,
who was, for fifty years, a constant attendant on its
delights: that stage, dignified by the magic talents
of Garrick, Siddons, Kemble, Henderson, Edwin,
Farren, Lewis, Young, and hundreds more, whose
" resistless eloquence " has so often been employed
on the boards of the theatre, in that best, and highest,
and nearly holiest of all offices,—that of teaching mankind to prefer virtue to vice, and reason to folly.

VISIONS, DREAMS, &c.

LIKE all persons of lively fancy, she loved such
discussions as were connected with stories of apparitions of the dead, omens, witches, and *devilry* of all
sorts; and in the course of her investigations, was

most instructive and entertaining; showing extraordinary intimacy with sundry strange forgotten books,
and great strength and acuteness of understanding.

In this way, a conversation, commencing in some
trifling narrative of superstition, was sure to terminate
on her part, with a philosophical exposition of what
seemed supernatural, and in some rich and well-
introduced anecdote. Talking of the warnings of
death, which all of the race of Bourbon were reported
to have had, &c., she observed, that the flights of
imagination were not confined to objects of vision,
but extended themselves still more unaccountably to
sounds; and that she thought there was scarcely any
one who had not experienced once, at least, during
life, an instance of what is termed a *call;* that is, a
conviction of having distinctly heard the voice of
a friend, then distant perhaps two hundred miles,
pronounce aloud the hearer's name. This happened
to Johnson, while a member of Pembroke college,
when he heard, in the voice of his mother, at the
moment in Lichfield, his name, Sam, plainly spoken.
But, according to his biographer, Boswell, Doctor
Johnson seems rather to have felt with more solemnity

on this occasion, than did Mrs. Piozzi, when talking
of such things. In reality, Johnson never had a
thought of examining matters of a preternatural character, with a view to rational solution; whereas, she
invariably did this, and explained them, agreeably
to her pleasant hypothesis, as the effect of waking
dreams.

She once told us of a vision she had, but which led
to nothing except the strengthening of her conviction
as to the cause; namely, the force of fancy, which will
engage our minds, sleeping or waking, while its power
over us shall prove as uncontroulable in the latter
state, as in the former. This spectral visitation took
place as she sat at an open window on a summer's
evening at Streatham, when she saw a trusty servant-
man belonging to her establishment, walking slowly
towards the back door of her residence, and without
acknowledging his mistress by smile or bow, though
apparently looking up towards her, enter the house.

She immediately after this ascertained that the man
in question was within doors, and had not been out.
This day-dreaming, as it may be termed, is common

to all, and the foundation of most of the ghost-stories, gravely related, and as gravely credited.

Dr. Johnson, she observed, was not far from believing in second sight, as connected with deaths, and other misfortunes; but to this Scottish privilege she always objected, as having in it neither merriment nor reason; and as being productive of nothing but a depressing foreknowledge of ill which could not be prevented: thus adding the horrors of apprehension to the evil of an inevitable calamity.

She repeated what she called, and what indeed is a well-remembered story on the subject of dreams, and which I think I have seen in print. A man accompanied by his friend, visited an ancient mansion, and there saw, among other things, the figure of a lion in marble, represented as open-mouthed and enraged. On beholding the figure, the man exclaimed "there's my enemy! I more than once have dreamed that I should owe my death to a lion." And so saying and smiling in scorn as he spoke, he thrust his arm into the lion's mouth. But within was an iron spike which severely lacerated his hand; and a mortification ensuing, he died in consequence. This, said she, was a dream by which not only superstition would have been alarmed, but from which good sense would have taken warning. I then mentioned an event in private life, not generally known, but which was reported as true, and is as follows.

A prelate of our church, much admired for his fine understanding, talents, and political liberality, was one day proceeding to take an airing with his wife in their carriage. Just at their setting out, their eldest son, a highly educated and most promising young man, rode up, and desired to be of the party inside. This the bishop peremptorily refused to allow, direct-ing his son by all means to remain on horseback, and ride at the side of the carriage. The youth for a moment remonstrated, but his father insisted, and was cheerfully obeyed. The bishop's lady then begged his lordship to tell her why he so resolutely adhered to his determination of not admitting his son to a seat with them; adding, that in a matter of so much indif-ference she wished he had yielded. But the father replied that he had not acted without a reason; for that he had been tormented by a dream the night before, when he imagined that he saw his son suddenly thrown from his horse and killed : and that through fear of thinking himself superstitious for the rest of his days, he had persevered in rejecting his son's request. The bishop had scarcely spoken the words, when the horse on which his much-loved son was riding, threw the young man to the ground, and he was killed on the spot. The unhappy parents, the father especially, grieved incessantly for their loss; and Mrs. Piozzi remarked, that, dreadful as was the penalty suffered by the unfortunate father, it was a just infliction on a person who had disregarded one of the grand laws in the code of common sense, which prescribes to us never to be obstinate in what is apparently not an affair of moment.

———

Having mentioned the fine likeness of herself, presented by her to me and mine, I shall here add the lines which accompanied a gift so highly prized, and which I preserve as sent, within the case containing this excellent miniature. We were at the time making arrangements for a very long journey.

" Bath, July 7th, 1817.

" While partial fancy's dictates you,
My generous friends, obey,
And keep my lifeless shade in view,
Companion of your way :

These features Roche's happy art
Has from oblivion sav'd ;
Your own, upon my faithful heart,
An abler hand engrav'd."

————

The reader may have discovered, from passages in her letters, that she entertained sentiments of gratitude, esteem, and genuine love for her husband, Mr. Piozzi. Often have I and others heard her avow these sentiments, and she repeatedly assured me that, in every respect, he was a perfect gentleman, and that no man could merit more of woman than he did by his deportment towards herself. It was, therefore, with a feeling of regret I read an expression used by Mr. Croker, in a note to his valuable edition of Boswell's " Johnson." In vol. iii., page 413, the editor refers " to sarcastic observations published against Mrs. Piozzi," on the occasion of what he terms " her lamentable marriage."

But can that occurrence in her life be justly so

called, which to her was productive of happiness,—
of that which we all so eagerly seek for, and so rarely
find? I am willing to believe that, in applying the
phrase above mentioned, the able and enlightened
editor did so rather in conformity to the tone of censure assumed towards Mrs. P. by the uninformed and
prejudiced multitude, than as speaking from himself;
because, in the progress of his arduous work as a com-
mentator, he has seldom missed an opportunity of
standing forth more as an admirer of her than as an
opponent; and, unlike the cruel and misjudging world,
has frequently done justice to the character of this
amiable, most accomplished, and distinguished woman.

There is another note introduced into Mr. Croker's
publication, which calls for a word or two of remark
on my part. In volume iii., p. 279, Malone is quoted
as terming Santerre "a detestable ruffian." I desire
to be thought incapable of attempting to vilify Louis
XVI., or vindicate the cowardly misereants who
destroyed him. The unhappy king was assuredly
foully murdered; but Santerre was, by accident, the
military servant of the powers then prevailing in
France, and was constrained to obey their mandate.
If the anecdote which I have repeated in a foregoing

page concerning him, be true, as I believe it to be, it serves materially to clear him from the charge of wanton barbarity in the performance of his dreadful duty. Mrs. Piozzi, who was personally acquainted with him, never spoke of him with the slightest share of harshness, as a member of society: nor do we discover in the records of those disastrous days, any authentic statement against him for peculiar atrocity, at a time when no one could be a revolutionary leader, without being, more or less, a criminal.

This is sufficient. I shall only add, that should what I have written communicate but half as much pleasure to others, as the writing has afforded me, they will have no cause to complain.

As to myself, I pretend to nothing but what is implied in the words addressed by Constant to Napoleon :—

"Je ne suis pas la Rose, mais j'ai vecu pres d'elle!"

And, if I have succeeded in producing a more alluring portrait of our friend than has yet been

given of her, it is because I have not been a copyist,
but drew from nature.

My chief aim was to exhibit a faithful, but not un-
favourable resemblance of one of the most extraordinary and agreeable persons it was ever my good
fortune to know; one, by whose unfailing kindness
and condescension I felt myself greatly obliged, and
highly complimented; and whose equal in most respects, were I still to live as many years as have
already passed over me, I might well despair of
finding.

The direful misfortune which occurred in the
family of a gentleman whose sons were unhappily
drowned at Weston Super Mare, during Mrs. Piozzi's
sojourn there, and which she relates in one of her
letters, brings to memory the unqualified praise she
bestowed on some beautiful lines addressed to these
beloved youths, and written by their fond father, but
a short time before his cruel bereavement.

Mrs. Piozzi's taste pointed them out to my notice;
and I indulge a melancholy pleasure in transcribing
them from The Bristol Mercury of April 26, 1819.

VERSES

BY

CHARLES ABRAHAM ELTON, ESQ.

ADDRESSED TO HIS SONS.

WRITTEN ON A VERNAL DAY, DURING CONFINEMENT FROM INDISPOSITION.

———◆———

Go, happy boys, on whose white foreheads, Time
Ploughs not the furrowing lines of human care ;
The Season, like yourselves, is in its prime ;
Pure as your spirits, breathes th' elastic air.
While languor my reluctant limbs enchains,
Race with the bounding lambs, as blithe as they ;
Listen the rustling hedge-bird's twitt'ring strains,
And wreathe your hats with primrose and with May.
The FATHER, whom by that endearing name
Ye know, and worship as Essential Love,
Stretched out yon azure vault ; and he, the same,
Lighted the sun ye feel, and gemm'd the grove.
Go, and enjoy the gifts his bounty sends,
And while ye sit by rock, or bank, or tree,
Think that with books, those ever present friends,
Time passes not uncheeringly with me.

R

VERSES BY C. A. ELTON, ESQ.

The same kind spirit felt within the wood,
In the wild violet's breath, or ivy's shade,
Is present with me in my solitude,
Filling the void your absence else had made.
Fancy, his gift, can lead me forth to roam
With you the hawthorn lanes and mosses green,
Or bring you back to my sequester'd home,
To tell the pleasant wonders ye have seen.
Hope, too, his gift, is whispering of the day,
When animating health shall set me free ;
When, where ye now are straying, I shall stray,
Climb to your cave, or sit beneath your tree.
And we shall bless that same paternal Power,
Who, still benignant, bids us smile or grieve ;
With wise privations heightens rapture's hour,
And never leaves us, though ourselves we leave.

BION.

THE END.

BRADBURY AND EVANS, PRINTERS, BOUVERIE STREET.

For EU product safety concerns, contact us at Calle de José Abascal, 56–1°,
28003 Madrid, Spain or eugpsr@cambridge.org.

www.ingramcontent.com/pod-product-compliance
Ingram Content Group UK Ltd.
Pitfield, Milton Keynes, MK11 3LW, UK
UKHW010338140625
459647UK00010B/679